The Wisdom of Wall

Robert,

I hope you can find something in these pages that resonates.

Best wishes,

The Wisdom of Wall

Ieden Wall

ISBN: 1548969362
ISBN 13: 9781548969363

Dedicated to
The Loving Memory of
Bella Wall

Foreword by Mark Breslin

When my old friend Ieden Wall contacted me and asked if I would write the foreword to his new book, I immediately said yes.

Then I found out it was a book of poetry. Trouble is, I don't like poetry. Or maybe I just don't like poets. Even the best ones are dodgy.

T.S. Eliot and Ezra Pound were anti-Semites. Emily Dickinson wouldn't leave her house. Delmore Schwartz and Sylvia Plath committed suicide. Even Leonard Cohen had the gall to die this past year.

I wanted to warn Ieden not to publish this book. The whole enterprise was just fraught with danger. But you know Ieden. Well, I do. And stubborn is his middle name.

So I picked up the galleys of his book and I started to read, carefully, so as not to disturb the universe. I didn't want to be another poetry statistic.

And you know what? The book has charm. The poems have grace. He makes you care about what he cares about. He drops into the dark caverns, without giving them short shrift and then shoots back valiantly into the light.

I shouldn't be surprised. I was a fan of Ieden's TV series, *The Dream Chaser*. But this is a whole different Ieden, up close and very personal.

Now, if I could just get rid of this strange cough ...

Mark Breslin is the founder of Yuk Yuk's, the largest chain of comedy clubs in Canada. He has produced for comedy legend Joan Rivers and launched the careers of Howie Mandel, Jim Carrey, Norm Macdonald and many other world renowned comedians. In 2014, The Toronto Star named him one of the most influential people in Toronto.

Author's Introduction

I have laboured for months on just how to welcome you to my first book.

I wanted it to be perfect. I wanted you to feel some of the magic I felt, as my pen was stroking the slightly crinkled sheets of paper into the wee hours of the morning. This book you are about to read is the result of countless sleepless nights where I was glued to my notepad (Yes, many of my best poems were born in real ink and on real paper). In a time where most writers live by their *laptops* and *iPads*, old-fashioned enthusiasts of the written word will be happy to know that I still compose on home-grown wood pulp.

So let me start by speaking about my Grandmother Bella. I loved my Grandmother as much as any grandchild can love a Grandparent. One of my favourite memories of her, is spending the night in her tiny one bedroom apartment, just talking about nothing and everything into the wee hours of the morning. And then after a marathon conversation, we would get ready to call it an evening.

My grandmother had twin beds in her bedroom, one for her and the other was the bed of my late Grandfather Harry. My Grandmother was very particular about who she let sleep in my Grandfather's bed but she afforded me the honour. If you understood how much she loved and adored her late husband, you would understand the true extent of this honour.

There is an image of my Grandmother that will be frozen in my mind forever. It's a picture seared into my sub-cortex. It's of her laying in the bed beside me with her lamp on, reading one of her favorite old-fashioned romance novels. I can still see her beautiful blue eyes as they trained onto the small print. As I awoke in the morning, I would pry open my blurred eyes, only to see her in the exact same position, lost in the same book that was completely irresistible to her. She loved to read and this made me love to read.

Since I was a very young boy, I have been keeping a diary of poems. From the time I was 12 years-old I was fascinated with the challenge of engaging readers in one page or less. A good poet can say more in 12 lines than a novelist can say in 500 pages. I am one of those odd guys who has always carried a notepad around with him -- everywhere -- never wanting to miss an inspired opportunity to jot down a poetic phrase. Carrying around a notepad has served me well. Often my quick chicken scratch on a park bench or a subway car has mushroomed into a new poem.

Part 1 of my book is a lifelong collection of poems. I am not a song-writer by trade. That said, my natural instinct has always been for lyrical, ballad driven poetic structure. It just seems to be the way the words float into my brain. I am flattered that my manuscript has garnered many requests from North American recording artists, to turn my poems into popular songs with original music. I look forward to working with emerging musicians, to take my words from the written page and transform them into haunting melodies and timeless songs. I can't wait to work with all of you!!

Part 2 of my book is my personal diary of wisdom. Being on my own at 15 years-old has afforded me a unique vantage point, upon which to refract a very puzzling world. The details of how I ended up on my own at such a young age do not matter. It was what it was. And it made me the man I am today. It made a book like this possible. That said, it was certainly not easy. While most of our friends were panicked over their acne and which party to attend on the weekend, my twin brother and I were busy trying to figure out how to pay our rent and come up with grocery money. My adolescence was marked with great hardship but it was during this time that I was able to start to widen my intellectual scope and build my emotional depth.

My twin brother Harlen has been an inexhaustible reservoir of support and inspiration in my life. He is a gifted writer in his own right and I look forward to seeing his amazing body of work published and brought to market. If I am wise, then much of that wisdom is a direct result of being a twin. That's the simple truth. Esoteric discussions and debates with my brother over the years have constantly challenged my beliefs and elevated my thinking to places I never thought possible. Thank You Harlen for making this book possible.

All of that said, I gladly hand over to you my personal diary of wisdom in *Part 2* of this book. I hope my insights can offer you guidance, clarity, comfort, revelation and ultimately a pipeline to many of the truths of the universe. Truths that perhaps, might have eluded you thus far.

Please enjoy both my poems and my pearls of wisdom. May you find the words that you need to hear. I thank G-d for bringing this project to fruition and may G-d bless you all.

Ieden

Part 1
Poems

Me to You

It is not me who writes these words
But I opened myself to receive
And then to become a vessel to say
What is in the mind and heart of
A much wiser being

It is not you who hears its truth
But you opened the book
And turned the pages to
Receive the wisdom of
Heavenly sages
As they communicate
Through me -- to you

The Way You Deserve

The world's left my heart tattered and full of holes
I want to light the fire again but I just feel cold
My own mistakes have left my body wrapped in scars
I want to break the bandages but I'm stuck behind bars

I was on the road to salvation but I got stuck in rush hour
The devil put me up for ransom but the deal went sour
My missed opportunities have left me full of rage
I want to love you but my anger has me trapped in a cage

I was convicted by jury for a million bad choices
My sanity was questioned for hearing too many voices
I was denied parole, bitterness sentenced me to life
I used to kiss with my tongue but now I only bite

But you would have loved me in my prime
I turned a dirty look into a heavenly sign
I made a servant out of time
Regret used to live next door, but now it's mine

And so it goes, this is my story
I am useless to a love so very young
For you need hope, of which I have none
If you have any brains, you won't walk, you'll run

My life has whisked by and in the mirror
Is the man I never wanted to be
I want to love you the way you deserve
But my face is someone you weren't suppose to see

I asked G-d

I asked G-d for the luck to achieve
Instead, he gave me the faith to believe

I asked G-d for great physical size
Instead he made me frail
So I would conquer with my eyes

I asked G-d for great riches
So I could mingle with wealthy faces
Instead he made me poor
So I would find wealth in deeper places

I asked G-d for comfort
So I would not be caught in the rain
Instead he made me suffer
So I could comfort others in pain

I asked G-d for glory
So I would be seen as a victorious man
Instead he cloaked me in failure
So I might learn who I really am

G-d made me strong, powerful and wealthy
But I never asked for any of it

Vegas

The plane lands on a jagged piece of neon
A scorching tarmac shows its cracks
While a clumsy hitman covers the facts
The ghost of Elvis Presley is back
In this town, every loser wants to be a winner
Every hooker wants to be a little thinner
There is a church beside every casino
Because Jesus loves a sinner
Around the table are anxious cries
But serenity lives in the dealer's eyes
He stands on a box, with a chip in the paint
With the hand of a sniper but the heart of a saint
The table is warped, a shape I've never seen
His hands look dirty but the table seems clean
Like Russian roulette, each turn becomes bigger
Greed and despair fight for the trigger
I came here for the big score, something outlandish!
Man, I love the rush but the pain, I can't stand it
Now I am broke, even my plane ticket just vanished
But I'll make it home, so help me I will
Just like Dorothy, I'll make it back to Kansas

Salesmen

The tanning salon sells four different shades of the sun
While an Eskimo down the road, sells ice on a bun
And the plastic surgeon sells you back your youth
While your lawyer goes to bed, searching for the truth
And the jeweler sells you love, wrapped in special gold
But it's your shrink who profits when the romance turns cold
And the newspaper sells you stories, a headline with a rant
But the paperboy forgot to warn you, the print was on a slant
And the cult leader sells you, a cool place to belong
He lets you buy on credit, but the payment plan is long
What are you selling?

Inside of Me

Who is this person inside of me
Who looks back in the mirror
Who is this person inside of me
Who acts like an ass
But is so sincere
Who is this person inside of me
Who hides in darkness
Hoping to shine
Who is this person inside of me
With such an evil grin
But eyes so kind
Who is this person inside of me
Who stalks me all night
With no remorse
Who is this person inside of me
Who courts me all day
But wants a divorce

Humility

Let me tell you the story about the man
Who couldn't say, I am sorry
He woke up in the morning
With the sound of regret ringing in his ear
On his way to work, he saw no traffic
Just guilt in his rear-view mirror
He knew his temper had ruined
That once tender feeling
But he couldn't muster the words
To do the special healing
A part of him wanted to turn the car around
Race home and say I am sorry
But the devil stepped on the gas pedal
Because humility has no glory
So he just kept driving
With his conscience hovering above
Wondering why he made a habit
Of hurting his one true love
She waited for those two magical words
All day by the phone
But he was frozen behind the wheel
Proud and all alone
His heart wanted to apologize
But his ego put up a struggle
So he just kept driving
Over the ashes and the rubble

Eventually he made his way home
To an empty house and a letter
It said the words, I love you my dear
But I deserve much better

A Conversation with G-d

When I was a child, you and me had a good thing
I said my prayers and I learned to sing
The songs that praised all of your ways
But then the rain set in, like a narcotic haze
I jumped ship 'cause the water grew high
You took my heroes, before I could say goodbye
And to you my Lord, I was a traitor of the highest order
I preached your words for a buck and a quarter
I used to call your name when there were lions to tame
And then I turned my back to dance with fame
Now I come to you, to renew our bond of love
I hear at the pearly gates they only push and shove
But I'll wait my Lord in the back of the line
For the times I was cruel, when I could have been kind

Get Me Home

Let me gather the revelations that never made it through the clouds
Let me gather the dead rebels who were a little too proud
I had a man in my corner who craved the sight of blood
I had a lover in my bedroom who couldn't love
I got a newspaper from tomorrow, with yesterday's news
I got a new-age musician in my kitchen who's sing'n the blues

Let me be the truth that would have set you free
Let me be the tattered noose, swinging from the tree
I got a penny in my pocket that survived the revolution
I got a politician in my wallet that says he's the solution
I got a lump in my throat and a chill in my bones
I got a compass in my satchel that's *got to get me home*

Let me find the 11th commandment that never made it to the stone
Let me find the calcium that never made it to the bone
Let me find the angel who spoke for me in court
Let me find the blueprints to the plan that Satan couldn't thwart
I found a candle still burning for the Emperor of Rome
It's only got a flicker but it's *got to get me home*

Let me find the romantic moment that led to my conception
Let me find the chromosome that made me the exception
Let me find the mystery man who's lurking behind the curtain
Let me find that moment when a G-dly nation became uncertain
I want the thug who turned the ringer off on my phone
It's about to die any second but it's *got to get me home*

9-11

The Towers whispered before the fall
We never asked to be this tall
G-d said, the fire will blaze
Today no fallen rain
The smoke will rise
With me to blame
Souls will wither
With hearts so torn
Mothers in heaven
While heroes are born
G-d said, evil will strike
Today no shame
The angels will fight
For a minute of fame
The towers cried
We don't want to leave the sky
And G-d spoke, You'll rise. You'll fall
But you'll never die

A Woman of the Night

She led me down the garden path
She looked like a question that I shouldn't ask
She told me to paint her while she was undressing
Every inch of her body left me guessing
Every pinch from her nails left me regressing
She saw fear in my eyes and this made her smile
A woman who delighted in seduction and fight
I was confused by her face, no compunction to trace
She was an angel by day and a devil at night
Her eyes told a million stories, none of them were true
I thought they were green but really they were blue
How many hearts did she crush with her glare
How many fingers did she let run through her hair
Her eyes were icy but deep down, she still cared
Just like you and me, she was stuck on a hijacked flight
Oh G-d, don't forget about the women of the night.

The Spotlight

Backstage
My palms varnished with sweat
Forehead acquiesces next
Dripping uncontrollably
Unable to contain my anger
For the love I didn't get

Standing behind the curtain
Limbs become numb
Now I am out of body
Looking down and all around

Eyes jet through a tear in the cloth
On my heart hangs the tag
The price I paid
The friends I betrayed
To take the stage today

The seats are filled with demons
Who stare with an evil eye
Still trying to sell me
What fame can never buy

Terrified, excited, but willing to confront
I walk towards the spotlight
There is no turning back

Light so bright, I can no longer
See the toxic faces
And the crowd looks on
Standing in the shadow
Of my dream

The Voice of G-d

His voice caresses with the morning sun
Beaming down, a gentle song
And now divinity has come

His voice wrangles in the wind
Gusting, spiralling -- sounds of discord
A raspy reprimand -- a punishment for sin

His voice bellows in the storm
Tacit anger gives way to irrational words
Grinding his teeth so we will conform

His voice withers in the rain
Each drop a little melancholy
His dejection soon to lift
Setting the stage for the sun's
Gentle whisper to return

Bitter Divorce

How dare you cross examine me
Without representation
Accusing me of drug abuse
Because of pupil dilation

The court of law is no friend of mine
You can kick and scream, my love
I don't have the inclination
And I have run out of time

How dare you call me a quitter
In front of our children
Who I sired in front of G-d

How dare you take my money
Seduce our priest
And then call me a fraud

How dare you say, I never loved you
With your hand on a bible
While our wedding photo
Still hangs at our church

You say you lost your soul
And don't know where to look
Well honey, you have a lifetime
To scour and to search

Sexy Lady

Sexy Lady,
If you are the kiss of death, leave me alone
If you are the jaws of life, break into my home
If you want my soul, it's on the endangered list
Poachers aim their guns, but they always miss

Sexy Lady, I might be crazy but when it comes to love
I'm not lazy. Oh there is nothing I won't do
To make love to you

If you need somebody to walk on, rest your feet on me
If you are broke, put away your wallet, my love is free
If you need a cover, I'll knit a blanket for you
If you want some gum, I'll give you something to chew

Sexy Lady, I might be crazy but when it comes to love
I'm not lazy. Oh there is nothing I won't do
To make love to you

If you want a devil, I'll put on two horns for you
If you want a courtship, I know how to woo
If you want a toy, I'll be your rubik's cube
If you want it old-school, I'll give it to you smooth

Sexy Lady, I might be crazy but when it comes to love
I'm not lazy. Oh there is nothing I won't do
To make love to you

If you want an animal, I'll take you to the zoo
If you want a cannibal, I'll eat you
If you want a husband, I'll say I do

**Sexy Lady, I might be crazy but when it comes to love
I'm not lazy. Oh there is nothing I won't do
To make love to you**

No Bad Questions

Why is every weatherman a pathological liar
Why does every ordeal feel so dire
If a King is impotent, how will the Prince get sired
Why in the nighttime does the devil always hire
Why does a piece of swampland always find a buyer
Why does hot air always want to go higher
Where does the fractured soul go to renew its lost season
Where does the curious mind go when there is no reason
Why are the eyes of a shadow always beaming
Why is the train to redemption always leaving
Why can the other sock never be found
Why does light travel faster than sound
Why do we trip over our own feet and blame the ground
There are no bad questions, right?

The Pond

I stand and look at my own image
In water covered in waste
Half a century looks back at me
With no love in its face

Weeds jetting up from what was
Once a perfect pond
Where the sun bathed its sorrow
And the stars looked on

I stand and look at my own image
In water so polluted by
Shallow love and empty dreams
By ghosts who defecated
In thy holy streams

Even the swans are no more
For they found a new home
To rest their heads

They grew weary and sore
For the loving words
That were never said

As long as I have You

If you want a Prince, then that's what I'll be
I'll give you a tour of the very best in me
I'll guard your heart with a rebel yell
And I'll stand up well, to a world that fell
And I'll rumble with your ghosts of yesterday
And I will break your false idols
That were made of clay
I'll go to hell and dance with devil
I'll hit him with my best jazz tap
If that's not his thing, I'll do some gangsta rap
Or maybe get'm with my old soft shoe
Something only Sammy Davis could do
I know I'll make it through
As long as I have you.

Auschwitz

I would think this is not real
If not for the pain I feel
As it hollows out my heart
And leaves just a vacuum
Where the torment once lived

I would think this is not real
If not for the smoke
That bellows to heaven
Burning the innocence
That was once mine
And the smiles that shined
Leaving a dark stain
On the perfect blue sky

I would think this is not real
If not for the children's cries
Their moans and groans
That travel from my ear drums
And straight through my soul
Sights too gruesome
For human eyes
Leaving me quivering
In shock that has no words

I would think this is not real
If not for the sound
Of the train
The beaten and slain
The murdered and maimed
Deafening silence
I will never be the same

Google Glasses

Hey, there is tall Robert James
Wow, he's on to wife number 3
His eyes look tired, a graduate of MIT

Hey, there is the lovely Doris Black
Powder blue eyes, wow, what a rack!
A crown prosecutor from Albany
I bet she's a talker in the sack

Hey, look over there, it's Greg Blair
Divorced with a restraining order filed
He wears his heart on his sleeve
30 years on Prozac, abandoned as a child

Hey, on the street bench, it's Don Juan
The great latin lover, what a great name
An electrician from Minnesota
A blue collar chap, with nobody to blame

The Pub of 1967

A lager that makes you stagger
Until you forget your name

A wine that makes you blind
And forget the reason you came

Welcome back to 1967

Today love is fresh off the tap
The kind that won't make you fat
Every lady is a little bit shady
But penicillin cures the clap

Dylan's on the radio
With the answer in the wind
The boys are in Vietnam
Paying for your sins

Dr. King is preaching
Like an engine
Running out of steam
And John Lennon is
Smoking up with Yoko
Because every profit
Has a dream

If You Know How

If you want to listen to my heart, lay on my chest
If you are into fine art, my collection is the best
If you are quick on your feet, I'll let you carry my gun
If you have a maternal instinct, I will make you a son
If you are willing to give your life, I am looking for a wife
If you know how to scale a fish, I'll give you my knife
If you can drive a stick, I'll give you the keys
If you can swing a club, I got plenty of tease
If you know how to touch, I'll give you lots of skin
If you know how to finish, I'll let you begin

My Name is Israel

When I was young I was bombastic, elastic
A man who could weave through traffic

When I was young I was erratic, ecstatic
A hard-core fanatic

When I was young I was invincible, unprincipled
I did things unthinkable

Like Jacob, I lied for a blessing
Without confessing the deception that
Ruled my mind

Like Jacob, I fought the angel
All night wrestling
And then I won back the blessing that
Was always mine

Romeo and Juliet

Love is a young man's game
And so is fame
So I'll break the chains of time
Just Like David Blaine

Love is blissful jaunt
And a trip to hell
Hey, the Romans fell
But cupid never lost his aim

Love is a connoisseur
And a raconteur
He can sing romance
And dance you into a trance
His charm will endure

Love is mystery
And a history of
Romeo's first day at school
It's an X-ray of the human heart
But Juliet was nobody's fool

The Dreamer

A Dreamer sees the beauty
Where there is none at all to be found
A Dreamer spots a flower in bloom
When there is only frost on the ground
A Dreamer sees the light
In the darkness of the night
And a Dreamer sees the victory march
When he's almost lost the fight
A Dreamer sees the sunrise
While he's standing in the rain
And a Dreamer sees the pleasure
While he's fighting through the pain
And a Dreamer sees a branch
At the very end of the rope
And a Dreamer sees the chance
When the world has lost its hope

The Grandfather
I Never Knew

My Grams says she fell in love with a poor man
Who carried his fortune in his heart
A man with two gentle hands, who peddled fur from a cart
She says she fell in love with the greatest Jewish Knight
A very soft and tender soul who became her guiding light
She tells me stories of a gentleman who wouldn't harm a flea
And when your name comes up, her eyes always water
But she won't cry in front of me
She says you left her alone to sleep in a bedroom built for two
But she kept your bed beside her, because for you, her love was true
And I want you to know, although you are not with us in body
You are still the leader of our clan
You haven't lost your stature, a giant of a man
I know you've been away and the family has been rearranged
But you are still a husband, a father and a grandfather
So nothing's really changed
And if I could do just anything, I would bring you back
For all the world to see, the man who stole my Grandma's heart
And forever holds the key

Amnesty

A sea of blessings
Yet of your life
You made a travesty

You threw away the
Baby with the bathwater
And then claimed
Amnesty

But to you my child
I do forgive
Your weakened
Heart and your
Fickle mind

For you are wild
Not like us angels
You think you see
But really you
Are blind

The Alcoholic

I am not here, nor there, nor somewhere in between
My soul is bare and I swear, it's like I'm stuck in a dream
I followed the path of many, to the land of plenty
I lost my money, every single penny
Poverty gave me back my wealth
Sickness gave me back my health
Loneliness helped me find myself
The bottles won't open and the glass won't break
I haven't drank for a year but my heart still aches
I could use some drugs but my pharmacist
Has only the names of the man I once was
Pills made me feel loved
Back to the place where everybody knows my name
Back to the place where I can take away the pain
My bartender aims his pistol
The round has already been bought
When I was young I used to carry a gun
But now I'm too old to take the first shot

Monk

I suppose a moth to the flame
Is so profane
To the man with discipline

I suppose a magazine cover
Is an evil lover
To the man with a double chin

I suppose a drowning beauty
Is like an unattended duty
To the man who can not swim

I suppose a chain smoker
Is like hardcore poker
To a gambler
Who still loves to win

The Promised Land

Bequeathed to me
The will to be free
To fight another day
To be the man that
I want to be

Bequeathed to me
A book of fire and light
A covenant with G-d
Of what is wrong
And of what is right

Bequeathed to me
The ear of The Father
The heart of The Son
The courage to fight
And the legs to run

Bequeathed to me
Over the horizon
The promised land
I'm a broken man
But on G-d's promise
There I stand

Reader

If I read your mind
Will you say I committed
A crime

Or will you praise me
For saving us some time

If I read your eyes
Will you deny it
And say I lied

Or will you call me your
Soulmate
And never say goodbye

Revenge

Bitterness,
You kidnapped my Father
People say why bother
To seek revenge
Well, I am that kind of guy
I read the bible
And it said in scripture
An eye for an eye
You think I won't find you
We all know where you hide
In the dawn of disappointment
Under a fly in the ointment
In the good intentions of a lie
And in the eyes of a sad goodbye.

G-d Speaks

Seek me with all of your heart, and all of your soul
Teach me what you have learned as you grow old
I wrote your story long before you were born
But it's still exciting to see it come into form

You can't surprise me but you can speak what is true
Like your very own Father, I love to hear from you
Your dreams are my dreams, so don't be blue
Run away if you like, but I will always catch you

Let Me into the Club

Let me into the club ...
I paid my dues
I even threw away love

I tripped out of the gates
So I crawled around the track
I was sold out by heaven
But I fought my way back

I don't have a penny
To my name
But even worse than that
I've run out of people
To blame

Let me into the club ...
I have been in the cold
For far too long
Even a lone wolf
Needs a place to belong

So Cry

If you want some blood, the needle better be clean
I lost my nerve, but I found my dream
If you want my heart, it's on my sleeve
I may be old, but I still believe
If you want my soul, I lost it at sea
The sharks are circling, but they don't fancy me
If you want some wisdom, then I'll be your sage
I can see the future, and I am not afraid
If you want a lover, just reach out your hand
I know I act like a boy, but I love like a man
If you want some intimacy, look me in the eye
I'll give you my soul, if you know how to cry

When I was Young

When I was young, I was such a fake
My mind was empty but I had lots to say
When I was young, I took'm down the garden path
Man, I really knew how to make them laugh
When I was young, I did whatever it takes
But now I am old and I regret my mistakes
When I was young, every meal was a feast
But now I am old and I just want some peace
When I was young, common sense couldn't stop me
Now I am old, I love to read but the truth is hard to see

The Pearly Gates

Pillars of granite
Stand higher than the eye can see
Alive in me
Dead as a tree
A light I have not seen before
Searching for the door
No panic now
Every man wants a crown
The gates will open
They must
It's all been discussed
And I have been forgiven
For my burning lust
My inability to trust
For my thick crust
From flesh now to dust
A panhandler at the gate
But I walk naked now
For Heaven can't wait.

Time is Blind

No King can rule forever
No matter how clever
For he will be overtaken
By those who were forsaken
By his dime

But his reign will be reclaimed
By someone with his name
Who thinks the very same
Because time is blind
Time is blind

And the slaves will misbehave
From the bottom of their graves
For their voices will be heard
Not left behind

So we must cry for the plight
Of those who couldn't fight
For a cause that wasn't right
Their heart was kind

The Prince, he was lynched for
Missing by an inch
The gory battle had been won
The King to crown the evil son

But salvation will be delivered
Probably by the river
To tender lips that quiver
And The Lord will shine

And The Lord will shine.

Mine

I must need you, to find the way to feed you
And I must become you, to overcome you
I must be you, to finally free you

For I am yours and you are mine.

The Past He Left Behind

Stella walks you to her tent
A place free of rent
As she starts to undress your evil mind
And then you see no flesh
Just her dark silhouette
That will confess, it's all been a lie

She'll ask you to tell her
Just before you smell her
What you left behind
For she knows you are guilty
And just a little filthy
And she knows the reason why

But knowing doesn't stop her
From flipping her hair
In such a way that makes you
Want to bare your tortured soul

To bare your tortured soul

Her eyes invite you under the covers
As her beauty promises to recover
The heart of every lover and the truth
In every lie you ever told

She'll ask you to come inside
Where no man can hide
From the horror and the shame
Of the man he became
While running
From the past he left behind

I'll Find a Way

I'll find a way, but it might not be today
So I'll wait for good old Father time
I know he'll walk my way

They say you can't keep a good man down
So I wondered if a man like me
Deserved the crown

Did my lies get into the hands of my ex-wives
Who felt that I ruined their lives
With the women I met in smoky dives

Did my sins catch up with me
Did they refuse to set me free
Did they kill the man I longed to be

Oh I'll find a way, but it might not be today

Did the bridge I burned, fall into the sea
Did the villagers drown, all because of me
Did the cat starve because I didn't climb the tree
Who do I pay for the games I used to play

Oh I'll find a way but it may not be today.

The Journey

Every lonely drop of rain, spells the name
Of heroes crying on heaven's row
They shall not wail, on sturdy ships
That sail valiantly, so far below
A boat needs no sun to take a run
It only needs the moon's glow

No light for ships that sail at night
No light for planes that cancel their flight
An idle stream gives weeds a chance to grow

Without water to drink, a camel can't wink
At the dehydrated fink who forgot to think
About the challenge of the journey

Men are strong but are often wrong
When telling their wives, they have 9 lives
For they know not when fate arrives

There are no good goodbyes
But the journey must be tried
Sometimes you'll stumble and
Sometimes you'll just glide
But the journey must be tried.

The Story of Life

We walk
We run
Until we get too much sun
And then we shiver and quiver
So hot we get cold

We talk
And we shun
And we get looked after by our son
And then we wither and quiver
And wonder how time
Made us old

A Call to the Weary

What does a man do when it's too much to hold in
And it's too much to let out
What does a man do
When he doesn't have the strength to shout

What does he do when he just can't face the pain
What does he do when the blood curdles in his veins
What does he do when the one person he loves
Stabs him in the back and leaves him in the rain

Oh this is a call to the weary soul
Who looks so young but feels so old
This is a call for those too scared to blink
The ones standing on the lip of the brink
The heavy hearts about to sink

This is a cry to the creator of all life
Please give them the wisdom to know
That there is a light beyond the day and the night
Please whisper through the wall of loneliness
So your soft timbre might uplift those faltering
On the other side of the the wall.

A View From Above

I jumped in my car,
I drove as fast as I could but every red light was mine
Sometimes we need to be late, to get there on time
Few are the runners whose waist hits the tape
Sometimes the man who falls and crawls, wins the race

I hopped on a plane that went 700 miles per hour
Praying that the engines would not lose their power
Looking out the window of the Lear, I saw above my fear
As I looked down to the ground, I started to produce a tear
The state of humanity sent cold shivers down my spine

I got a glimpse of the *anarchy* cloaked in *order*
I saw a charitable man being duped by a hoarder
I saw the armies storming the border
I saw a giant attacking a man 10 ft. shorter
I saw an *honest* priest selling a nickel for a quarter

After mere seconds, I had to turn away
I could simply not bear to ingest how the humans
Had sunk to the bottom of the ocean where even
The sharks swim with more grace and dignity.

He Will Be Found

Mozart set the stage for classical rage
But Beethoven was the sage
He composed without any sound
Every boxer wants to step back into his youth
One punch away from finding the truth
Ali lost his mind but he never lost a tooth
Every flower wants a second bloom
Every woman wants to seduce you with
her perfume
Howard Hughes lived in a mansion but
He never left his room
Don't cry for a hungry child
The messiah will be here soon
Van Gogh moved his brush in a special way
But nobody wanted to pay
And Jimmy Hoffa built a union one day
The devil asked if he could join
And then Jimmy he lost his way

He will be found.

I Think Therefore I Am

Plato lived under the wing of Socrates
King David cried to G-d on his knees
No piece of wisdom is given for free

Freud said, "blame it all on your Mother
If you end up with an evil lover
Don't trust the first woman you see"

Stalin said, "an emperor rules with an iron fist"
But Gandhi said, "a passive rebellion
Is sweeter than an erotic kiss"

Jesus said, "let the first stone be cast
By the man who hasn't sinned"
But Dylan said, "the answer is
Blowing in the wind"

René said, "I think therefore I am"
Mandela said, "a man must take a stand"
The Wright brothers said,
"First you have to be in the air
before you can figure out how to land"

Shaw said, "Youth is wasted on the young"
But Solomon said,
"Life and death is in the power of the tongue"

My friends it is not what you tell others
That will destroy your health
It's what you tell yourself.

I think therefore I am.

My First Dance

I walked over and asked Jennie
Do you want to dance?
I knew she would say yes
For 7 years her smile did suggest
That one day she would acquiesce

They say a dance is just a dance
But when you're twelve years old
It's the birth of true romance

She smiled and then struck her serious face
Which hung over white lace and girlish grace
And we walked onto the floor
And together we opened a door

Earnest, alive, shy, reluctant to share her own
Exquisite beauty, and allow a man to
Get a glimpse of who she really is
Where she lives, Where she hides
Why she cries, The love in her eyes

We started out far apart, with my fingertips barely
Touching her thighs, I looked away because ...
It is not easy to look your first love in the eyes
G-d knows I tried

The song went on and the closer I got
It became really hot
Dripping with sweat but moving closer
Such a moment can't be bought
There is no price, no good advice
Your first dance never happens twice

The song was almost over
But I got just close enough
So she could rest her head
Our hearts pounded out loud
But words were never said

They say a dance is just a dance
But when it's your first
It's the birth of true romance

The Arms of Love

The fists of anger always hit under the belt
I was sequestered by guilt for the love I never felt
I was deprived of sleep for the promises I didn't keep
I am haunted by the enemies I always wanted to beat
Compassion is easy to rent, but it's hard to own
A lie yells in a crowd but the truth speaks alone
Saying I love you is easier on the phone
We are all trying to find our way home
Bandits spend years planning the great caper
Money can't buy love but it sells a lot of paper
Evil sucker punches you on the chin
The arms of love hit between the eyes
Because that's where the real light gets in

Sexual Healing

In the dead of the night, she came to me with a knife
She hugged like my Mother but she kissed like my wife

I wasn't scared, my heart was prepared
A man waits for this his whole life

I don't like a mystery and I am not into history
But this woman wore the faces of so many I knew
She slipped her gown down, and put her arms around
My bewildered heart
She put her hand all the way in
She knew what to do

I put my tongue on her spine, and drank her like wine
It was a tryst in the vineyard
And the grapes were fresh off the vine

Entangled in her beauty, her fragrance got me under her spell
I asked about the scars on her arm and the blood on her hands
She said, every woman has a secret to tell

I had a feeling her soul needed healing
As I looked at her body, in the mirror on the ceiling

I probed for more and I touched a nerve that she didn't deserve
And then she gave me a warning
She said, make love to me -- for tonight I am free --
I'll share my story in the morning

Don't Forget Your Brother

Scripture says, I am forbidden to rue thy enemy
For in his dichotomy, I learn so much about me
One day a friend, the next day an enemy
But we learn from everybody we see
A lover will uncover your battle scars
And blow down your house of cards
For love will take you to that
Secret place
That you simply can't erase
Sex can be an awful hex
But making love will set you free
Your lover will pull the covers over you
So remember to be kind to your brother
He'll bring you back to the truth
He won't let them neglect you
He won't let them forget you
He'll make you laugh so hard
You'll forget that you had the blues
Because that's what brothers do
For love is pure when there is no woman to woo
Never let a lady come between the two of you

The Truth

As the truth travels hands, it can't stand
To the authenticity of where it came
It loses its sharpness, it's depth, it's breadth
You're half alive but you're still in the game
Heart surgeons are cocky and glib
Attorneys are good with a fib
And poets alway seem trite
Am I the only one wondering:
How did Edison see anything
While he worked through the night
As a mosquito lands in an unknown land
West Nile killed the boogie man
And that's the truth.

Poor Van Gogh

Every gypsy lives off of the fat of the land
The cactus plant shows us how to live in the sand
The gladiator knows only one man can survive
Superman never forgot to set his alarm clock
Because Clark Kent worked from nine to five
Every firefighter understands the power of the flame
And every actor wants his moment of fame
A doctor wants to heal the broken and the lame
And every preacher wants to do the same
Every charming thief wants to steal your heart
But that poor Van Gogh could never sell his art
Poor Van Gogh.

The Sands of Time

Every pitcher looks down from the mound
We all run away to be found
Love hangs its hat in a small town
And tomorrow keeps time around

What happens when the sands of an hour glass
Fall onto the hands of time
Why does G-d send a profit
To go down in his prime

We live. We sigh. We laugh and we cry
But few have the guts to give love a second try

We run. We crawl. We stagger and we fall
Even if you leave the phone off the hook
You won't miss the final call

Be that as it may, your soul is here to stay
Every tomorrow is one dawn away
From becoming today
We all have our demons to slay
But the price has already been paid

The final act of the play is written
In the stars and etched into clay
It will never arrive yet we live in
Constant fear that it's on its way

We live. We sigh. We laugh and we cry
But few have the guts to give love a second try

The Poet

We come into this world so homesick
For a place long forgotten
Like the naked branch on a winter tree
That longs for it's autumn

No pistol to start the race
No Sherlock Holmes to solve the case
How do we know what's here to stay
And what's a passing fad
Some say Beethoven was a genius
Others say he was mad

Every army's after more land
By the direct order of a lesser man
The war is lost but the battle has been won
G-d bless the poet, he never carries a gun

He turns dark into light
Death into life
A fence into a stand
A coward into a man
And he does it all with no blood on his hands.

You'll Never Lose

I stood on the edge of the abyss -- and I almost slipped
My iron constitution had a 30-year run and then it dipped
The line between overconfidence and terror is just a blip
Remember, even the righteous angel can be tripped

I went to an orgy in Malibu that they said was BYOB
100 naked women had their eyes glazed over me
Sodom and Gomorrah had no door and had no key
Every citizen wanted out but they lost their will to leave

No cult has ever preyed on the man with self-esteem
For the man who owns his own soul, the devil shall not lean
You will never find mercy in a land you've never been
The holy grail isn't at the start or the end -- it's in between

Every man was on the path to enlightenment, until his ego grew
Every story's got a villain and a hero and a man just walk'n through
Robin Hood was a thief and a donor -- and baby, so are you
Stay close to the pedestal in your heart and you'll never lose

You'll never lose.

Value of a Poem

I ask myself: What is the value of a poem?

It demands a noisy world to sit alone
In its own deafening silence and meditate
On the beauty that once was so enveloping

It forces men of con, to find a new pawn
In the game of running from pity and shame
So they might travel light again
Shine bright again
Fight the good fight again

It points a broken woman to the mirror
To see her own irrepressible beauty
That dwelleth in the great beyond
Past her eyelashes and car crashes
Past her collisions and poor decisions

It points fallen men
To a time way back when
The moon did shine its spotlight
On their lofty dreams
And filled the holes in their souls
With the eternal hope of the loyal profit
Who knew success was soon to arrive

It shall lift the burden
Of those who are uncertain
It shall animate the hands
Of a good surgeon
It shall tame the beast
Inside a priest
And shall restore
Order to the human soul
And lead her all the way home

That is the value of a poem.

If You Want to Know Me

I want you to know me
Not the softness of my skin
But where I really begin

Not the spark in my eyes
For this is still not me
Just a convenient alibi

Not the fullness of my smile
Spirited though it may be
It's only here for a while

Not the timbre in my voice
Hypnotic though it sounds
My real voice is still
Waiting to be found

Not the manner in which
I make love to you
Sensual though I am
It takes a better plan
To know me as a man

Tribute To Leonard Cohen

Critics say
He could turn a rhyme
For he was once sublime
But over the years
He lost his shine

Well I read the bible
And it clearly said
A prophet is never
Past his prime

A Jewish boy from Montreal
Who left his home to answer a call

The call to fame
Destiny gave him a kiss
He made it to the A-List
But he never played the game

The call to heal
His words gave weariness
Some dignity -- he said
It's OK to be broken
If that's how you feel

The call to glory
His story was our story
And in a world of illusions
He gave us something real

And so now they mourn
From Paris to Rome
From Jupiter to Mars
And back here at home

For the man who writes
In greater heights
In heaven now
A hero who recites
The unforgettable poem

Still Waters

The wind blows, sometimes weeds can grow
A river eventually leads to a dam
Behind a great woman is a grateful man

The sun bounces off *still waters*, with G-dly precision
Leaving the sun's rays to ricochet back
Through the haze and the floating clouds
Past our devoted angels who fly in a secret realm
Between earth and heaven

Still waters contemplate how to rejoin the
Mellifluous flow of earthly streams
That lead to the rivers -- and the lakes -- and oceans
And back through our dreams

The eye of the storm, ratchets up its galactic fury
And where the the gentle whisper of G-d's spirit
Hovers over the synchronized tides
Waiting for the world's final cry

Blessed Be The Name

Blessed be the one who sacrifices what is most precious to him
The one who dives into the water but cannot swim
The one who risks it all and goes to war
The one who gives his freedom, so you can have yours

Blessed be your Mother, the one who carried you for the full nine
The one who watched for you when you were blind
The man who was forsaken, but is still so kind

Blessed be your teachers, who instilled the values that got you here
The heroes who pick you up, when you are consumed by fear
The angels who keep you on the road, when you can not steer

Blessed be the name of the Lord, who has commanded us to
Wash our hands
The one who allows us to flourish in foreign lands
The one who goes by the name: I am that I am

Immortality

We are all on the outer crust of this fallen star
We all sit alone at the end of the bar
Time moves along and sings its song
The sun cast its ray and it burns mighty bright
But even it was not designed to stay
This world at its core, an obsolescent wonder
Even thunder will eventually go under
Blue Jeans will also exit this galaxy
And the truth we know will prove a fallacy
This in no way kills the immortal part of you
Which no professor can teach
No telescope can reach
No contract will breach
And no sage can bequeath
For eternity is well beyond what you can see

The Unfitted Tux

We all were born into an unfitted tux
It hugs us tight around the heart
But nobody will notice, with a little luck
We all hide behind a scary mask
We all run from a noble task
We are all the beggar, holding up our sign
Hoping to get into somebody's mind
Get past security, to the front of the line
So we might feel like a glorious piece of star dust
Even a righteous man has a moment of lust
We all want to be at the water cooler in the morning
And hear our name discussed
We all want to throw a better man under the bus
We all lose our scruples for women that moan
Just when we start to feel good in our tux
We find out it was just a loan

Hard to Create

We all want to think we are the cultural elite
We all wear stinky feet
We all put on cologne for our dream date
We all put on our hood and run from fate
We all put destiny on our calendar
But we don't have the patience to wait
We all want to sleep in the penthouse
And then we complain about the rate
It's easy to destroy but it's hard to create
It's easy to talk but it's hard to relate
It's easy to glut but it's hard to satiate
It's hard to love but easy to hate
No perfectionist wants to delegate
It's easy to say please but hard to say thanks
Eventually every gun will shoot blanks
Nobody wants to climb up the ranks
It's so much easier to rob a bank
Some things are meant to be
Some things you'll never see
The best things in life are free.

The Messiah Will Be Here Soon

Every boat is sinking
Every strategist is thinking
G-d never blinks
The house always wins
The Captain can't swim
Shakespeare was tragic
Houdini knew magic
Howard Hughes was stuck in his room
The depression led to the boom
The messiah will be here soon
Armstrong did a soft-shoe on the moon
Every witch rides her broom
Every test is given too soon
Every seed of lust wants to bloom
The bus to enlightenment has no room
Don't worry
The messiah will be here soon.

History

In a world of laziness, initiative is the trump
Every Cy Young pitcher made it through a slump
If all deeds eventually lead to greed and corruption
What does an innocent boy put his faith in?
Well a Mother's love is a good place to start
And if that's not appealing
The sistine chapel has really good art
Moses said to the Pharaoh, let my people go
Pharaoh said NO, you know the rest
And if you don't, it's never too late to learn
For history is a chameleon
It wears a new face every century
But it shall return
It shall return.

The Mountain

The poet stands on the mountain with a cape
A girl on the ground below falls to rape
It's all enshrouded behind the arms of the trees
Delila brought a grown man to his knees
Man's machinations against man
Make filth out of earthly splendours
We all cry foul, yet we are the worst offenders
Maybe World War III will be on hypocrisy
The downtrodden will vacate their pubs
Fetch their clubs and eradicate aristocracy
If I was a smarter man, I might cave to depression
I might join the meek and fight disproportionate aggression
I might chastise the tough guys, for emotional suppression
I might call out the evolved nations, for their regression
But my intelligence is fair and I am too tired to care
So I sit and grapple with my simple question:
How can society advance when the righteous among us
Have lost their glutton ...
And the devil has his henchman with his hand on the button

If Love Was A Soldier

If love was a soldier it would storm the enemy without warning
It would make love all night -- and again in the morning
It would fight for the loftiest ideals
It would keep tyranny on its heels

If love was a soldier it would rescue loneliness in the still of the night
It would ride in like a cavalry to fight for what was right
It would capture despair and cut off its hair
It would inspire those who don't seem to care

If love was a soldier it would pray for its victims and their family
It would trade in its aggression for something less manly
It would imprison intolerance and throw away the key
It would kidnap hatred and throw him into the sea

If love was a soldier it would carry a pistol but turn the other cheek
Its face would look scary but its heart would be meek
It would put the devil completely under siege
It would stay in the field and never fatigue

Instructions for Happiness

Make the effort to eat organic
Think more about the planet
Smile, it will instantaneously change everything
Even if your voice sucks -- let yourself sing!
Know that regardless of the year;
It's always a battle between love and fear
Be kind to the haters, even if they're wrong
They're the ones that will make you strong
Learn to release useless information fast
Don't dwell on the pain of the past
Stop envy before it makes its pitch
Know the lesson is always in the glitch
Strive for more but be grateful for what you have
Give yourself a few minutes to be sad
Give yourself a few hours to be glad
Remember that *expressing* is good but *pursuing* is bad
The *process* is joyful but the *outcome* is always mad
Nobody cares more than your Dad
Treasure the time that you have
Don't judge -- just love
Remember to wear a glove
Forgive those who trespass
Know, this too shall pass

Every Man

We are all afraid to win but we all hate to lose
We are all poets when we find a muse
The smoke will blow and the dust will settle
Drug testing stole the olympic gold medal
Here today and gone tomorrow
Every man is alone in his sorrow
Become the change that you want to see
Don't forget to cut a second key
Because G-d laughs when you set a plan
Every teenage boy wants to be a man
But few boys have the guts to take a stand
We all live in castles made out of sand
No snowflake wants to land
Every man wants to bed his female friend
Every man longs to be a boy again

Love is Eternal

Every path has already been taken
Every word has already been spoken
We came into the world a little broken
Be that as it may,
Yesterday has something to say
Oh how I used to love to make you smile
We all wear a crown for a while
Even if we don't learn, the pages will turn
My mind is tired but my heart still burns
It's a race against time but the hands are stuck
The angels sigh when we call it luck
Someday I will see you again
And we'll feel the same way we did back then
Because love is eternal

Sleepless

We all want to raise the bar
The truth has to travel far
Burglars sleep in the day and work all night
A thread of dust travels light
Destiny never cancels the flight
Every delusion thinks it's right
No dentist wants to have a shark in his chair
Every judge thinks he is fair
Every fabric has a tear
Every woman wants you to stare
Every genius is mad
Every clown is sad
The proud man has poor vision
Only those who care
Make the right decision
Fear is heavy
Love is light
Care is sleepless

When I Was Young

As I get older, the truth runs after me more
It's like a pebble in my shoe
That's so hard to ignore
I used to want money and fame
Now I just want someone to ease the pain
It's hard to blame when we're all the same
Oh how I miss my youth
When I was too short to see the truth
When I could grow back a tooth
Now I am just left with my roots
I daydream too much about way back when
I miss my childhood friends
I dreamt one day my eyes would meet the sun
It looks so breathtaking now
But it looked even prettier
When I was young

Yesterday Has Lots To Say

Tomorrow is speechless but yesterday has lots to say
If you listen too much, she'll make you pay
She wants to dash your dream
A theft carried out in the infant hours of the day
So audacious is she, that she will blindside you
In your greatest moment of certainty
Stopping you dead in your tracks as you
Stand at a crossroads

To break away from her grasp, you must understand
What motivates her and what is her endgame
She wants you to stay the same
Never play the game
Be seduced by blame
To waste away by the bay, while your gifting
Rots with the wild oaks, as the cold autumn
Overthrows the withering summer

Many greater than you have danced with her
And lost their way: Her name is yesterday
Her bedroom eyes and succulent lips
Give way to her her voluptuous figure
Orchestrated perfectly by her hips
For she appears flawless in every way
She'll bring you a beer and twirl her tongue in your ear
And insist that she is yours and you are hers

By contrast, *tomorrow* wears a modest gown
She lives on a dirt road with no grass on the ground
She never makes a sound
She can't captivate you for her eyes are hidden
In the blinding light of the sun
And her body is masked
By a long garment of mere chance
And the tiniest glimmer of hope
Yesterday and *tomorrow*
Both meet you at your crossroads
Good luck.

King Without A Crown

I had a dream on the way to school
That life was a play, and I was the fool
That I was the King with nobody to rule
When I was a Prince, I was pretty cool
But when I became King, I became cruel
I hid in the palace, because my enemies were many
I was surrounded by gold but I didn't have a penny
I slept on the finest silk and bathed in the purest water
I had no heir to the throne but how I loved my daughter
Royalty played me right out of tune
I didn't know much, so I would just assume
I had a garden full of roses but they refused to bloom
It was the life I had always dreamt of
I had too much of everything
But I didn't have love

The House Of The Lord

I walked in with only my soul to bare
In every other house, I was beside myself
But I found comfort there

The pews were empty, just me and the Lord
Beneath the room tone I heard only silence
The phone rang from heaven
My ringer was off, but I heard the call
Sometimes our tears need a place to fall
And I found it in the House of The Lord

The sanctuary was dry, but outside it poured
I went to the ark and put my hand on the scrolls
And I spoke the words of The Lord
I am not a religious man but it struck a chord
It felt like I had been here before
A man fighting a war, longing to be restored
Every man will one day face his own sword
But I found my grace in the House of the Lord

Sometimes our heart needs a place to cry
And I found it in the heart of the Lord

Childhood Love

I shouldn't be thinking of you
I got so much to do
It's been a lifetime
I guess my heart's not through
Loving You

I miss the way you made me blush
I have seen so much
I guess it's hard to let go
Of a woman I could trust

Love is so foolish
It travels through time
I guess it's true what they say
It's patient and blind

We were so young
But the feeling was true
I flirted with love many times since
But it was never pure --
After you

When We Were Young

We all sing happy songs out loud, but we whisper the blues
We lit up every star in the universe, but never blew a fuse
How I miss your embrace and your sweet taste
I think of all the time that went to waste
How we got so lost and then found our place
Every now and then your fragrance blows my way
My tongue wants to speak but it has too much to say
It means so much more looking back
But life fades memories to make room for now
I would have made love to you if I knew how
But my body and heart were too young
Sometimes I am sad at what has become
But man did we laugh together when we were young

The Crisis

You don't know it now friend, but *crises* has come to save you
It's a hero disguised as a villain and it's love is true
Sitting underneath the frazzle of your fear is a sweeter sound
In months, you'll rise again but first you need to be broken down
I know you're scared but sit still and listen to the angels wail
Your train was heading off track but you're back on the rails
You were misusing your ink and authoring another man's tale
You were wandering away from the footprints of your trail
You were ignoring the love letters and opening the junk mail
You were trying too hard to do it all alone
You let the devil's receptionist answer your phone
But the times, they are changing and the cards are re-arranging
Don't be scared by what you see in the mirror, it's just a lie
Remember, the ugly metamorphosis allowed the caterpillar to fly
You can't see it now but you are being reborn, take it from the wise
Nobody likes a crises but it didn't fall on you by mistake
Oh G-d has a heart and when his children are lost, it really aches
But he's got you in his hand and you're perfectly safe
He's going to get you to dry land -- he'll do whatever it takes.

Like a Man

I woke up this morning, with this feeling inside
Like a silly little boy, who just wants to cry
I had you in my grasp but you fell through the cracks
It's easy to fall in love but it's so hard to make it last
With our bodies in heat, we took passion to its peak
Our will was strong but our hearts became weak
We made love on Egyptian cotton
The sheets were so very clean
We took our fingertips to parts of the body
Where love has never been
Your hair is still on my pillow, each silky strand
Every time my face brushes against it
I feel like a man

Fresh Start

My mantle is empty, the photographs have lost their way
Yesterday they spoke to me, but today they got nothing to say
I am looking for a fresh start, something that smells like spring
I am looking for fine art, a landscape that knows how to sing
I am dancing alone now, to Beethoven Number Nine
I am looking up to the heavens for a heavenly sign
I buried our first kiss, just under the tree
I threw our first touch, right into the sea
I am traveling light now, into the open road
For everything there is a season and a time to let go
Autumn is a killer, but Spring resuscitates the rose
Outside my window, I hear the voice of my wife
My mantle is empty but my window is so full of life

Rocky!

Every sauna is heated by the broken pieces of a boulder
Every con-man is crippled, from looking over his shoulder
Moses struck down an Egyptian, under the glare of the sun
Some say it was a murder, some say it was a hit and run
Some lose their life from a cork in the eye
Some get run over by a train and never die
Where have all the good men gone
Maybe they're hiding in the hour, just before dawn
Mother Theresa cared for a leper and still had perfect skin
Some men fix their own fight and they still can't win
Ali dislocated Foreman's jaw and then opposed the war
Rocky was always on the ropes but he came back for more

One Holy Mess

Pull the plug on this sinking ship
We are all walking with a broken hip
We are all talking with a bloody lip
We're limping through the darkness --
And there are no candles to be lit
This is one holy mess

I heard a Rabbi say:
It's hard to find a decent man to bless
I heard the Pope say:
It's hard to find a humble man to confess
I heard the store owner say:
It's hard to find a sunny window to dress
This is one holy mess

When does this circus hit the road
When can we lessen the load
The good men are being taken
The demons are being awakened
This is one holy mess

They're dying by the thousands
Just starving to the bone
Help is one call away but --
Nobody's picking up the phone
Babies are crying all day
For the chance they never got
Politicians are lying about
The war that was never fought
This is one holy mess

Every policeman is on the take
The paramedics are running late
Chance is at war with *Fate*
There is no time to waste
They're closing Heaven's gate

Passing Glance

I heard about a haunted house on the coast of Greece
Eighteen ghosts were arrested for disturbing the peace
I heard about a healer, who would wander all day long
And I heard about a harp player, who lost his song
I am just a broken man, searching for a little shelter
A woman with an icy stare who might let me melt her
I'll tell you man, it gets so lonely here in my gaping mind
People tell me, I'm looking for a love that's hard to find
But tonight, I just want a woman's body on mine
In every smoky bar, I always look to the back of the room
Because love often strikes, in the dark distance of chance
Like an old time movie, it starts with a passing glance

The Good Guys

I did thirty years for a crime that wasn't mine
The release papers never got signed
I got a neck brace so I couldn't hang my chin
Worry kept me slim
The devil begged me to join him
But I resisted because
The good guys always win

In my youth I was a gold medal dreamer
These days I am bronze winning pessimist
The silver is still up for grabs
So I'm working on my abs
I am on a mission slim
The good guys always win

I am looking for the one who pulled the rug
The man who sold me the drugs
The optimist who never pulled the plug
The easy life was never my friend
But I found my moment of zen
The good guys always win

I am coming back like the plague
I drank the magic potion
I'm rising from the ashes
Like poetry is in motion
Because,
The good guys always win

An Inconvenient Truth

The oceans are rising
The big companies
Are downsizing
The bad guys are getting
More enterprising
And us fools are buying
Everything we're sold

We used to delegate
Now we just meditate
To the sound of a
New age violin
Danger's com'n but the
Music is too loud to
Hear the siren

I work for minimum wage
But I have come of age
I put my reading glasses on
And the fine print says:
We've all been conned

There isn't one single candle
Just a sea of neon phones
An army of malignant bones
The angels are coming to collect
All the outstanding loans

Satan is binging on appetizers
The best he's ever had
Our seeds are being engineered
By some monkey in the lab
And our grandchildren are
Stuck picking up the tab

It's showtime my friends
The chicken has come
Home to roost
Even the new President
Can't distract us from
An Inconvenient truth

The Bad Apples

The world is being run into the ground by a few bad apples
They live in seclusion, so they won't be hit by the shrapnel
They design their machinations, on a format called Word
The documents are bleached, and then they're fed to the birds
They got the sheriff in their pocket, and they run above the law
They raise their own cattle, and they eat their steaks raw
They have their own bomb shelters, all stocked to the hilt
Their roses live in greenhouses -- while ours just wilt
They don't believe in Jesus but they go to midnight mass
They don't know how to drive but they decide the price of gas
They think that G-d fell asleep at the wheel
Heaven stamped the envelope -- and their fate has been sealed

Mars

I heard swampland is going cheap on Mars
I heard here on earth, cars are driving cars
We're going into the future, haunted by the past
We're popping pills for the love that didn't last
Maybe I will dance in the open meadows of chance
Maybe I will sail with you in the still rivers of France
Wherever our eyes will meet, the angel of love will open the skies
So our souls can ascend -- with the truth of yesterday -- and the lies
It's much easier to run and chase after fun
Than to put beauty to bed and have your lover by your side
But we're going into the future, with dirty air and flying cars
If we lose our grip on utopia, I'll see you on Mars

G-d

My words are trying to reach a place that can't be reached
Still there is beauty in the quest, in each moment that I meet
For in each moment, I draw closer to thee
And in drawing closer, I feel things I've never felt in me
The depths of sorrow
The hope of tomorrow
As my soul awakens, I understand why you can't be reached
You have perfectly concealed your face
So the stars might fill the empty space
And like lovers in the night, we might long for your embrace
For you desire our longing and not our touch
Longing in our trials
Knowing it's all worthwhile
Knowing there is a light beyond the sun
Knowing there is a fight to be won
And so you are slightly out of my reach
You are the victor that can't be beat
You are the fate I long to meet
You are the lesson I want to teach
But you can't be reached
In the still of the night
The floor of heaven creaks
And echoes the sound of your feet
As you walk on the clouds and imbibe the passionate longing
In the heart of every lover who reaches for you
And only you.
The Lord our G-d.

My Dear Sorrento

In the undertow of despair, my heart found its repair
In the brevity of the moment, I learned how to care
I winced at the morning when it looked back at me
It's eyes had a shade of blue, I had just never seen
Sorrento, how you filled my heart with joy
Sorrento, how you made me feel like a boy
Your sweeping water views, that saw right through
Your rugged cliffs, where the winds of change blew
Oh how you made my mind come alive with
Dancing images of splendor and replenishment
How you made my heart revive with dear Anna
Who gave my slouch the hand of accompaniment
It's so true that each and every land has its own
Enchanted beauty, living far beneath its soil
It rises up to embrace those who come to it in toil
To you my dear Sorrento, my heart will be loyal

Find Me

I went to Vienna, to find some better definition
I went to Athens, on the wings of a premonition
I've been talked about for my deeds
I've been hollowed out by my greed

I went to the Holy Land, to search the earth
For my roots
I went to the island of despair, to save a man
From the blues
I've been taunted for not wanting to try
I've been haunted by the reason why

I went to Venice, to learn how to row
I went to Sydney, to see what was below
I've been gambling with my unborn child
I might be spiritually bankrupt
But my income taxes have been filed

I've been all across the world.
And I am still trying to find me.

Date with Destiny

In the middle of the night, destiny called on my business line
He was a smoky baritone, who claimed I was on his mind
I was convinced it was a 3 am prank, payback for some
Fun I had when I was young
He told me that the call was certainly not a joke
And he had no time for fun

I asked where he lived, just to make sure he was real
He said he lives in the highest courts -- beyond repeal
He said he lives in the nerve-endings -- too numb to feel
He said he lives in the blind spot -- as we turn our wheels
He said he lives in our deepest wound -- that won't heal

I said, your voice is clever but it's your eyes I want to see
Then I'll know for sure that you are my destiny
He said I am what I say I am
I am the ribbon blowing as you cross the finish line
I am the ounce of courage that you can't seem to find
I am the joy that comes after you've cried in sorrow
I am the magic moment in your final tomorrow

For I am your destiny, now listen to me
Let go of the past and do it fast!
If you need some help from G-d -- then just ask
Get your eyes away from the shoulder
Push out your chest and get a little bolder
Don't put off your dream another day
Put your chin up and be on your way
There is a lot more I could say
But that's all for today.

Good With The Bad

We all want to party with the VIP folk
But none of us want the second hand smoke
We all want to go on a midnight binge
But none of us want to repent for our sins
We all want to live a fairy tale
But we can't handle the hate mail
We all get married for the security
But we get antsy under lock and key
We can all see the fungus on our toes
But none of us can see in front of our nose
Everyone wants to go on the rollercoaster
At the town fair
But nobody seems to like soiling
Their underwear

Serendipity

I met *Sorrow* in the park, on an empty bench
With cedar chipped and peeling away
Rotting from its exposure to the inhospitable
Elements and horrible neglect

I met *Serendipity* at sea, staring at it from
A tall-ship, as it winked at me through the
Rugged tides, that did not abide by any
Laws of order; completely unpredictable
Containing an endless array of ways to
Push us to the shore

I met *Joy* in a dark valley on the island of Japan
A few days before I became a man; it never
Swam and it had no plan; it came in the rising
Sun, on the wings of a monarch butterfly
Fluttering about, whimsical and effortless

I met *Hope* in a dark cave in the Holy Land
Beneath the bedrock of G-d's temple; it had
A voice that whispered; subdued by the
Unrelenting cycles of history but not
Completely vanquished, as it refused
To dance into the Jerusalem sun

A Better Man

I used to tend to the garden all summer, under the sun
Until one August day, my green thumb became numb
I went to the Doctor and he ran every test
They even hooked wires up to my chest
The tests gave no answers, just more questions
More fingers became numb, which left me guessing
I went to my shrink to see if it was all in my mind
After months of therapy, I was still in a bind
Only now my whole hand was numb, and I was miffed
I started to realize that a hand is truly a gift
I mean what is love making without your fingertips
Who is your lover, if you can't touch her lips
What is a hug if you can't grab her hips
What is a son, if you can't pat him on the back
What is baseball if you can't hold a bat
What is a gift if it can't be wrapped
What is a romantic moment, if you can't tip your hat
One day I woke up and I got my feeling back in my hand
I stopped hiding in my garden and I went into the world
A better man.

To Make a Difference

I met a man who wanted to buy back his youth
I met a man who almost died for the truth
He stood short on his feet but long in the tooth
He said he would search for more
And go look for a cause to fight for
And go look for a woman to die for
He said he would use his wisdom to inspire
He said he would use his virility to sire
And go into the city and teach the lessons of life
And go into the city to heal poverty and strife
Young, wise and well suited, he would be rooted
In his quest to make a difference in a world
Paralyzed by indifference

Casual Sex

My heart was naked but my body was dressed
My body was cursed but my heart was blessed
She carried a gun and I had no vest
I failed her expectation -- but I passed my test
She had hoped to kill me with kindness and
Then shoot me down with a round
She had a silencer but I heard every sound
It was hardcore romance, with a wide city view
I was hungry for love, I bit more than I could chew
The air tasted stale but the feeling was new
It was a storm of sexual pleasure,
Under the winds of inclement weather
With the heat giving way to thunder and light
Under the covers was a fight for my life
My body was naked but my heart was dressed
My heart was cursed but my body was blessed

Abraham

Fear beats a drum and it runs from the Lord
Love lifts a guitar, and it strums the chord
David played the harp when Saul became bored
But David was the one with a heart for the Lord

Isaac loved his boys but he could only choose one
They both knew a blessing was soon to come
The decision was made from high above
Over the heads of brotherly love

Abraham left his land, on G-d's command
He broke the idols and left the pieces in the sand
Every boy must leave his Father to become a man
Oh Abraham had such a gentle hand

Long to be

How I long to be pure
To be naive enough to
Believe in a cure
How I long to be sure
The way I felt when
My eyes met hers
How I long to be at peace
The tranquility I felt
When life brought me
To my knees
How I long to be me
Like when I was a baby
And there was nobody else
To pretend to be

Life is Absurd

I ask you, what is more absurd:
A tycoon who takes sleeping pills and still tosses and turns
Or the man who sleeps under the bridge, free from concern
The priest who embezzles from the broken and sad
Or the con man who donates every last cent he has
A religion who bows to a Hebrew man as The Lord
Or a religion that tries to convert his people by sword
A heart surgeon who faints at the sight of blood
Or a pig who turns out to be allergic to the mud
A mercenary who swims all day with the sharks
Or the same guy who goes to bed afraid of the dark
I ask you, what is more absurd.

Singing From Galilee

I heard in Jerusalem, there's a hole in the sky
And a mountain where death goes to die
The ghost of Abraham is gone now
But the Dead Sea is still alive

I heard the sea of Galilee has lots of weeds
Her shores brought the demons to their knees
Her fish had many mouths to feed
Her pages gave illiterate men
A reason to learn to read

The angels go to Galilee to bathe their feet
Her undertow is where good and evil meet
Oh Jesus walked on her surface
And his disciples fell to their knees

David wrote the songs, that the Lord so adored
Yes he was a warrior but his pen was his sword
David took down a giant, the victory was in hand
Our King was strong -- but he was just a man

The Table Has Been Set

A big ego is easy to bruise
A little love is hard to lose
Right and wrong are always confused
At the crossroads, you must choose
In motion, your path looks cursed
It's a road many have traversed
Nothing new under the sun
Life is a timeshare
It's favourite guests are
Ecstasy and fun
Don't ponder this world too long
Every conclusion you have is wrong
But doing what is right, will offer
Your journey some light
Be mindful in your sorrow
Hope is setting the table for tomorrow

Remember to Buy

I wore a blue collar, for a white collar wage
The public called me a fraud
But the inmates called me a sage
I got sentenced for life for being afraid
I kicked and screamed but I still came of age
They foreclosed my house for the hand I never played
I could be bitter but it's not my way
I go to worship but I am too proud to pray
I just keep talking when I have nothing to say
I was on my way to heaven but I fell in a pot hole
The doctor said my arch is good but I lost my sole
My real estate agent says, why rent when you can buy
My dealer says, why settle for a buzz when you can get high
Sometimes I wonder how I got here and where the time went
But then I have a few drinks and it all makes perfect sense
I missed my lottery ticket because the check was never sent
If you can, remember to buy and not to rent

My Gallery of Art

In a secret place in my heart
There's a gallery of art
And you're my Mona Lisa, babe
You're the lottery I didn't play
You're the stock I didn't trade
You're the love I never made

Thieves come to steal yah
In the middle of the night
It's a recurring theme
Jealous dames try to rip you
Right out of my dream

People say I am sentimental
Because I pine for your perfume
With my knees against my chest
Like a baby in the womb
Sweet visions of you, babe
Keeps me in bed until noon

You're still stuck in my head
The way you took the final shot
Maybe love is a sticky web
And we both got caught
But you're still alive my love
In a secret place in my heart
They all come to see you
In my gallery of art

Bases Loaded

I need to move but my feet are cold
I found my groove but my soul's been sold
I have lots to say but my story's old
Time to repent and then reinvent
Destiny's on third and I'm at the plate
I have a 7PM rendezvous with fate
And I am a lifetime too late
Time to clean the slate
And bring those runners home
My guardian angel's on the phone
Raspy and talking a little smack
He says, I lost my hands
And most of my fans
Have left the stands
But I know I can still deliver
Like I did in my youth
Tonight I am jogg'n all the way around
Just like little Babe Ruth

Midnight Friend

I am reaching for my pen, to help you rise again
Everything made to break, was made to mend
Let me be your midnight friend

I've been where you are and it can get dark in there
Sometimes it takes your soul to bare, to light a flare
And to learn again -- just how to care

Sometimes I think we are here to lose our way
To talk, until we have nothing to say
To spend, until we are too poor to pay
To fight, until there is no enemy to slay

And then to finally be left alone with our own
Tearful soul -- and to comfort this neglected friend

Every storm is born from the calm of the water
And to surrender its fury to the will of the Father
If it was not worth your while, he would not bother

So in your fear, and through your tears
Remember this:
I don't know where and I don't know when
But you will find your strength again
Take it from me, your midnight friend

Never Grow Old

I prayed for the strength to take you to that place
Where lovers quarrel and then embrace
That place where shame finds its grace
Where tender lips get touched
And the mystery of love, shows its face

I prayed for the courage to let you walk away
Pondering the words I couldn't say
Haunted by a dream that went astray
Sometimes, all we can do is pray

I prayed for the wisdom to understand loss
To absorb love's hidden cost
To walk through hell, with my story to tell
To drive its highway and never get lost

And I prayed for the strength, to carry a heavy load
Up the mountain and through the cold
On life's lonely road
To carry our love to a place where it would
Never grow old

You are More

You are so much more
Than hopes and fears
More than the body that
Lives in your mirror
You're the gust on the mountain
That blows at the peak
You're the rainbow after the storm
That your arm can't reach
You're the breath of the almighty
Who refuses to speak
You're the sigh of the elderly
Who says she's too weak
You're the cry of a baby
Who just wants to eat
You're the virtue of patience
In the back of the line
You're the will of a hero who
Shows up -- just in time

The Desert Came Alive

We've been traveling far
Guided by a six-pointed star
By a covenant and an ark -
And a promise -- That whispered
Through the dark

Sent to all corners of the Globe
Fate spoke with a bitter tone
But we got back on the road
And we started to walk home

We were haggard we staggered
A nation that was scattered
But we had a promise to return
And that's all that mattered

Oh there were dark days
When the sun went away
But through the foggy night
Our six-pointed star
It always lit the way

We wiped the tears from our Mothers
And the blood off our brothers
We got beaten and smothered
But we always recovered

We got burnt by the flames
We got tortured and maimed
And we broke down and cried
But our faith, it never died

And in the eye of the storm,
Our nation was reborn
And the desert that died --
Well it came back alive
It came back alive

We couldn't believe our eyes
It came back alive.

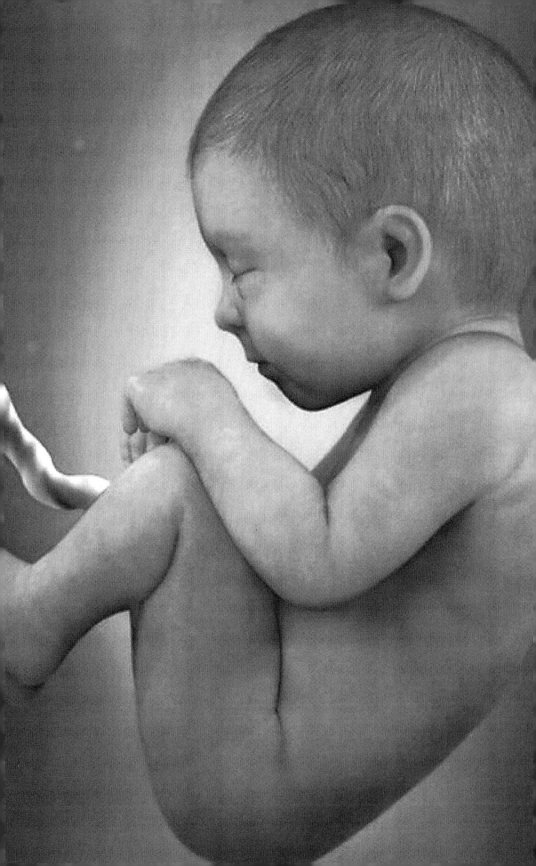

Early Childhood Memories
(a poetic look at life before life)

People call me overly sentimental because I pine for my Mother's womb
It wasn't extravagantly big but it seemed like there was just enough room
The weather was always pleasant, in fact I don't recall a drop of rain
Although how reliable are the memories of a fetus with half of a brain?
So what did I know really, I mean I was completely wet behind the ears
In fact I was wet everywhere, fully submerged, for three quarters of a year
Looking back, it was my first 5-Star hotel, the womb was my corner suite
I spent the first 3 months trying to figure out, why I had two arms but no feet
Eventually all of my limbs came and just before checkout, my penis grew in
I looked down and realized, there was a genetic lottery and I didn't win!!
In month nine, there was a flood, only G-d forgot to tell me to build an ark
It was a storm the weather man had not spoke of and I was stuck in the dark
I heard a voice that said, take me to the hospital, my water just broke
I heard another voice say, go in the car and I will just put on my coat
Eight days later, I remember waking up from a nap, to find some old man
Draping over me, with what looked like cooking swizzzors in his right hand
And much to my shock and astonishment, this frail old man proceeded to cut
Off my foreskin. He was smiling while he was doing it. Then he started
To laugh very hard. Then he looked over to my Mom and said, "It's all done,
he may need some plastic surgery when he's 5 - but all in all - I did the best
I could with what I had to work with."
Prick! These are my early childhood memories.

No Love To Be Won

When I was 40 years old
My Daddy came to me and said,
Son, your dream is running out of time
You gotta let it go, get on with the show
While you still have time--

I said Dad, I have an angel
He's just a little behind
He's working his way to the front of the line
He's got to pull a rabbit out of the hat
I know -- but he doesn't mind
Our watch is broke but his runs
In G-d's time

My Dad said son,
You got no reason to hang your head
Most people with a broken leg
They just stay in bed
But you got up and tried
And then we both cried

I said, Dad but I feel I'm getting close
To a place that can free us both
From the sadness that took us down
To the joy we never found
Because Daddy it's so true
That my dream was going to be a gift
From me to you

Then my Dad cried. He cried.
And I asked him why?

He said Son, I cry because
My dream was also for MY Dad
For the time I never had
For the hero who hid his wounds
For the man who left me too soon
For the man, I knew was the best
For the man I laid to rest--

And we both cried.
And we both cried.

And then my Daddy's Dad
Appeared up in the sky
And we both looked up, he was alive
We tried to fight the tears but we could only cry

And my Grandpa said Jacky,
Don't be fooled, your Daddy never left
I've breathed with you, in every breath
I covered you, when you needed rest
I stitched you up, when they broke your chest
I was there, when there was nobody left

So boys, chase your dreams just for fun
Because there's no love to be won
Between a Father and his son
There's no kisses to be found
There's no clock to be wound
There's no victim to be crowned
Love is never lost but it can be found

So boys, chase your dreams just for fun
Because there's no love to be won
Between a Father and his son
There's no beginning and there's no end
When it comes to the love
Between a Father and his son

You're In Heaven Now

You're finally in a better place
Where everything will go your way

You'll know everything your lover
Meant to say
You'll know the reason your Daddy
Couldn't stay
You'll know who set the price
You had to pay

You'll know why a child
Suffered through
You'll meet the angel
Who guided you
You'll know -- now --
You got nothing to prove

You'll know why love is
Hard to find
You'll know why women
Change their mind
You'll know why
Love is often blind
You'll get all the answers
You couldn't find

Oh it'll be OK 'cause you're in heaven now
You made it out of town, with your thorny crown
Step on a cloud and take a look around
At the pretty pictures and the perfect sounds
Take a jump Leonard, you won't hit the ground
You're in heaven now

Faith Delivers

We all love fingers through our hair
We all love to eat cotton at the fair
We all meet the face of temptation
Sooner or later, we miss our station
Every train eventually goes off track
Every road eventually leads back
We all fear the unknown
We all reap what we've sown
Love is all around you
You need a lie to see the truth
The ego just wants to refute
Every heart is fragile
Every dart is agile
Love never dies
Hope always tries
Faith delivers

On The Edge of Here

Fast forward the tape to me being great
Would you? I just don't want to be late
G-d please just give me the date
I promise I'll have the patience to wait
But not knowing is eating away my flesh
I feel sleep deprived from too much rest

I know the teacher never speaks during the test
I know the preacher never preaches in jest
I know the bleachers never see the best
But my destiny wasn't born to rest
I lost my sword but I'm still on this quest

All the Ghosts have disappeared
I like the face I see in the mirror
When you think I am worthy, just whisper in my ear
I'll be standing on the edge of here

I'll hitch-hike, if you point me to easy street
I'll walk barefoot, if you cushion my feet
I'll ride a bike, if you protect me from the heat
I'll take on city hall, if *The Man* can be beat

All the Ghosts have disappeared
I like the face I see in the mirror
When you think I am worthy, just whisper in my ear
I'll be standing on the edge of here

I stopped for a drink and the waiter said victory was near
I tipped him big, so he would say what I needed to hear
Sometimes we have to pay a cheerleader to cheer
Sometimes we have to slice an onion to shed a tear
Sometimes we need a weaker lens to see it clear

All the Ghosts have disappeared
I like the face I see in the mirror
When you think I am worthy, just whisper in my ear
I'll be standing on the edge of here

I figured it all out,
I know why my headlights get stuck on a deer
I know why love was caught in bed with fear
I know why malt loves to swim in a beer
There's a hundred voices stuck in my head
But I know which one is sincere

When you think I am worthy, just whisper in my ear
I'll be standing on the edge of here

Big Break

My climax is collecting dust
My paranoia is starting to trust
Courts been adjourned for 20 years
The jury's got nothing left to discuss
Do I get my break or am I a bust

The poet said, unrewarded genius is a cliche
The lifeguard said, there's no sharks left in the bay
The server said, there's no hors d'oeuvres left on my tray
The angel said, every dream lives to see another day

Now which dude deserves my faith
Which clown is holding the ace
None of them have a trustworthy face
I heard the prosecutor wants to close my case

You got to tell me man, did I make the cut
You got to tell me man, did I have the guts
Did I score big in the final round
Do I get to wear the golden crown
The angels say the song of victory is blaring
But I can't hear a sound

Did the dragon I slayed get up again
I'm starting to think he might be a friend
How many deaths do I need to cheat
How many ghosts do I need to defeat
How much pride do I need to eat

My climax is collecting dust
My paranoia is starting to trust
Courts been adjourned for 20 years
The jury's got nothing left to discuss
Do I get my break or am I a bust

A Better Road

Seduce me with your point of view
Introduce me to the broken part of you
Don't worry, I'm a little broken too
I got a skeleton in my closet that speaks the truth
His teeth are straight but his tongue is a little loose
Infuse me with the wisdom I always lacked
Point me away from the haunted road that takes me back
And to a better road.

The devil in me churns, but the sage in me yearns
Shoo me away from the flame that wants to burn
And towards vigilant ears, that only want to learn
I propositioned the goddess of love but I got spurned
I called Mother Teresa but she was all out of concern
I waited 100 days to reclaim my youth, but I missed my turn

I got supplanted to the balcony of life
G-d wanted me to watch the angels do it right
I got sent to a monastery to find my wife
Sometimes we're in the wrong place at right time
We all get stuck on the yellow tape around a crime
And sometimes an evil spirit has a beautiful mind

So lead me to the news stand that has the winning ticket
If there is an envelope that reaches heaven, let me lick it
Let me lay in the field of revelation with the crickets
Let me rise above the protest, I'm too tired to picket
If the elixir is still scorching, just let me take a sip
If my debt to society has expired -- I want the paper ripped

Seduce me with your point of view
Introduce me to the broken part of you
Don't worry, I'm a little broken too
I got a skeleton in my closet that speaks the truth
His teeth are straight but his tongue is a little loose
Infuse me with the wisdom I always lacked
Point me away from the haunted road that takes me back
And to a better road.

Parting Thoughts

I went on a witch hunt to find the love I never got
I got pale from sitting in the shady part of the lot
I sunk beneath the gravity of my morbid thoughts
I got tired of eating the burnt pieces on the bottom of the pot
I got bored of fighting the fights that I had already fought
I felt cowardly for never practising the lessons that I taught
I felt wasteful for never using the love that I bought
The best sleep I ever had was on a cot
There are no posers from high above
There are no bed sores on the wings of a dove
There is no vacation spot for the sun
There are no u turns in the barrel of a gun
We're all born with a loaded tongue
Genius will never rest
Prophecy will never guess
Put your faith in faith
It's the only thing that will get you through
This awful mess

Perch of Love

Take me through the disappointments
And to the sorrow that never left a trace
Unclench your fist, the fight is over my dear
Love is taking you to a better place

Suspend me from the height of your embrace
Let me know how your tongue really tastes
My heart is full for you
And I don't want a drop to go to waste

I know you know my weakest point
I know you know where my bone meets my joint
You've got my anatomy memorized
And you've got my senses mesmerized

You've got my enemies hypnotized
And you've got my dreams almost realized
Take me to that place where pain and pleasure meet
Under the moon's dancing eye

Let me be your prisoner in captivity
Baby I don't mind the chains
I am ready to surrender to your notions
I am ready to let you butter me in your lotions

We've been due from the moment our eyes first met
Our pupils exploded, inside the dry flesh became wet
Show me to the perch where you nest
Show me to every inch of courage you have left
I'll give you my trust and my willingness
And you can do the rest

This Ain't No Riddle

Regale me with your hopes and fears, both deserve a shot
Let me hear the gun brandish, just before it cocks
Let me bless the ground that you're about to walk
Because even though you think you're ready -- you're really not

Every man who thinks he can run above the law
Well, he's one bullet away from getting caught
Every expert needs to learn the lesson that he taught
And every man's trying to get, what he's already got

Half of of me wants to soar with the eagles
And half of me wants to keep both feet in the sand
Half of me wants to ditch this place
And half of me doesn't really believe I can

Oh every man's a King when he's flying in his Lear
And every man's a bigger King, when another man's fishing on his Pier
But no King can outsmart the beggar
Because sitting on the throne is fun, but to sleep on a bench
You really need to be clever

Folks, I didn't come here to twist your mind with a riddle
From my mouth comes the truth -- even if it dribbles
Too much will make you sick -- and so will too little
A virtuoso plays the violin but a hack, he only fiddles

Too much foreplay will only make you crippled
And too much thrusting will only make it shrivel
The sketch artist solved the crime, from just a scribble
Acid always kills, so be careful where you widdle

Hey, we're all punching a clock, on the assembly line of life
Maybe we're all a little wrong -- and just a little right
But here's the truth and trust me, it ain't no riddle
Sometimes a depressed man, just needs to be tickled.

Holy Spark

Let me know where you want me to go
And I'll run my fingertips so slow
And I'll touch you in a way that makes you burning hot
And I'll take you on a tour of you, just in case you forgot
Together, we'll find the right spot

Let me hear the child wail, just before it talks
Let me hear the door creak, just before it locks
Baby, I've been dreaming of us getting lost in the dark
If there is a flood, I want you and me alone in the ark
When my skin touches yours, blood rushes to my heart

Through every part of life's madness, our love has endured
Underneath the toe curls and the heaving breathing --
There is something really pure
Our ecstasy is a lifelong ailment
And face it baby, there's just no cure

You could be in another universe, I would tunnel through the wall
You could jump from heaven to hell and I wouldn't let you fall
You got me where you want me babe -- now it's your call
I was never a greedy man, but when it comes to you, I want it all

My friends say to me, release your grip and let this one fly
But I was captured by my own bliss, as it reflected in your eye
The wise nomad said a holy spark always dims in the night sky
But he never once saw it die.

The Poet Man

Mr. Poet Man,
They sent us to you to help us understand:
Why the water is overflowing and calamity has hit our land
To help us understand why a dead whale washed into the sand
To help us understand why the child is starving, from near and afar
While a tycoon spends his obscene abundance on twenty-five cars
Oh Poet Man, they said a wayward wise man is who you are
Don't let us down we have traveled too far

Mr. Poet Man,
They said you could help us to understand:
Why man turns a deaf ear to the heavens and to his fellow man
Why bravery and fear met in an the alleyway -- and bravery ran
They said 'twas the Emperor who ruled in ancient Babylon
But when the poet left, the truth was gone

Mr. Poet Man,
They said that deep in your hazel eyes lived the golden light
They said you could make a white shark lose its ferocious bite
And then spin a rhyme and turn a minor wrong into a major right
They said that you could take the stammer out of the meek
And that you could insert the brawn back into the weak

Mr. Poet Man, tell us now:
How do we take the tribal nature out of man
It's bringing famine to our land
How do we take greed out of the human heart
It's ripping our planet right apart
The angels promised heaven would soon descend
They said the broken and the lame would walk again
Oh Poet Man, what is a human soul really worth
If a pregnant woman says the pain is not worth the birth
We need your words, sage and swift, and ready to lift
Don't let us down, we have traveled too far

Oh Poet Man,
Come out of hiding and preach your words
Set the broken wings and speak life into the birds
Make sure the selfless beacons get what they deserve
And that the aristocrat will join the beggar by the curve
And finally, oh finally,
The lacerated victims to saunter through the palace
And then be served. And then be served.

Part 2
Pearls

A dream is a precious gem that hangs from the necklace of your soul. If you should lose this jewel, look deeper into your soul and you will find other ones; and maybe you might even retrieve the one you thought you lost.

The quickest way to realize your dream, is to help someone else realize their dream.

But how great is the human animal, I ask myself? Still one of the few species on earth that kills its own. Yet his potential to do good is unlimited. So despite his inability to live up to advance billing, he walks on the earth's soil with the promise of the most spectacular shooting star.

If you have to sell your soul for your dream, it was likely never your dream. We often chase the dreams of those we love the most. Be sure it is your own heart's desire that you covet. Painful to wake up one day and realize that you paid a heavy price for a dream that was not even yours.

It's a good thing G-d conceals the price you will have to pay for your dreams. If you knew the cost in advance, it is unlikely you would pursue these ambitions.

The two greatest illusions of your life are *Yesterday* and *Tomorrow*. Regret yesterday if you wish. Plan for tomorrow if it makes you feel better. But know this: To the extent that you can accept, embrace and ultimately confront *Today*, is the extent to which you can succeed. For *Today* is the most powerful reality you will ever know.

In life, we are tempted to wait until we feel strong enough. We are tempted to wait for the right time to conquer. But who are you to measure your own strength? And who are you to wait another second to conquer? THE TIME IS NOW.

Precious few are the people that don't experience rejection and loneliness. How you interpret *rejection* and *isolation* will in large part determine your character and your fate in life. Understand that every Prince and Princess returned home to the palace on the rocky road of rejection.

Everywhere you look there is is eye-candy for the ego. And for a second or two, this world might fool you into thinking that your social status and material wealth have actual value. The things you will take with you into the next world, carry little honour in this world. But know this: In the world to come, your only currency is, how much love your soul carries and how many souls you touched with your love.

Our immediate "heart" response to a gift of any sort has nothing to do with the gift itself. Our response is always a reaction to the "inspiration" in the sender's heart, that made the gift possible in the first place. Because life's greatest gifts are expressions of true love, these gifts are not easy to receive. They can only be fully received if one loves himself.

To put blame on another person for your plight in life is like a dog who foolishly bites onto his owners stick, thinking that it is the stick who is hurting him and not the owner who wields the piece of wood. There is a G-d. Take up your hurts with him -- not your neighbour.

The universe will always give you back what you are willing to give it first. It seldom offers an advance; rather it demands your trust and faith to believe that it will deliver. Without this trust you are stuck in a stalemate with the cosmos and G-d himself.

At the first blush of success a wise man will travel back to the streets of humble beginning. For he knows that his earliest successes and his earliest failures, made his eventual success possible. A humble man goes back home and says Thank You.

Many humans abandon their roots because one's roots often represent a place of struggle and pain. And revisiting that struggle can make a person feel vulnerable, disempowered and susceptible to the pain of the past. It is perfectly natural for a human being who has overcome a great obstacle in their life, to fear some sort of regression or relapse. Be of great strength and make the sojourn back to the roots of your pain. For you are a new person now and it is impossible to be at the same place twice.

One of the highest callings in life is to return to your origin of trauma for the purpose of comforting, consoling and healing others who are going through what you did.

When one is driven by an uncommon passion to do something, the important question is always *WHY*? If the *WHY* lines up with G-d's will, the *HOW* will manufacture itself.

When you feel wronged, your *EGO* will whisper, an *eye for an eye*. Be of great strength and shout back, *this is the great lie*. For every quarrel ends in regret and regret lingers like smoke in the sky. And though a punch feels great at the time, the thought of regret tortures the mind.

My friend, do not let the eyes mislead you or your heart deceive you. Do not covet the grass on the other side of the fence. For you could inherit a nice lawn with a home rotting at the foundation.

Forgiveness

The battle of forgiveness is an epic war between you and the dark forces that live within. My friends, be of great courage and fight these battles with all of your heart and soul. I will repeat -- fight these battles with *ALL* of your heart and soul. For the dark forces will be unscrupulous in manipulating you to think that by not forgiving, you are punishing the other person. When in reality, by not forgiving, you are literally eating away at your own flesh.

As the human *INTELLECT* soars, it will inevitably outsmart itself, leading its owner to the depths of despair. Once this happens, it must promptly acquiesce to the *HEART*, the man who was always supposed to have rein.

The true brilliance of this world is the way it hides its precision and flaunts its chaos. The true majesty of G-d is to carve his face on every image the human eye captures, and yet to remain completely invisible to its gaze.

G-d's light doesn't shine to you, it shines through you. You are here on earth as a vessel for this light. To the extent that you can remove anger, hatred and fear from your heart, is to the extent that you can shepherd G-d's light. This is why you are here.

We live in an electronic age. Information comes in fast and furious. Opinions and interpretations come in even faster. We are tempted to arrive at judgments of other people through pictures, videos, blogs and instant messages. However, until you are face-to-face and eye-to-eye with another person you are a million miles away from knowing who they really are.

To acquire intelligence, one must be willing stand up as a fool. For we live in a world where the answer is only a button away. Yet a wise man knows that true understanding can take a lifetime. Never confuse a swift answer for intelligence. And never confuse intelligence with understanding. To *know*, takes very little effort and even less time. But to *understand*, is to voyage through many storms that will seemingly never end. So then we can conclude that to *understand* one must have extraordinary hope, faith and patience.

My precious child, I am sorry if this is an inconvenient truth: Every child of G-d will eventually end up at the pearly gates. For the 'loving genius' who created all things, wastes nothing. Surely he would not cast away a human soul. However some souls will endure excruciating anguish as their soul travels to the most high. Some souls will ascend to heaven, floating blissfully on a cloud. When we refer to *Heaven*, we are speaking about intimacy and proximity with *The Source (G-d)*.

Be certain of one thing my child, the angels who tend to the heavenly gates, deal in only one currency: **LOVE**.

The furniture of the ego; monetary wealth, social status and superficial accolade have **NO** value as you stand at the entrance to heaven. Your only currency at this point is: How kind you were, how much love you shared and how many people you inspired to be loving and kind.

A great man works tirelessly to achieve success and instead of hoarding his wealth, he shares it without reluctance. For the Lord delights in a King who shares the precious gems on his crown with his lowly servants. Every King knows very well that by giving away part of his crown, he risks one day being dethroned. This is the measure of a King.

The line between self-confidence and over-confidence is sometimes thinner than a thread of dust floating in the air. Please remember that a self-confident man confronts the world with a true belief in his value and abilities. Whereas an over-confident man exaggerates his ability and worth to cover up his insecurity. The world cleaves to sincere confidence. Conversely, the world salivates at the chance to humble the eyes of the haughty.

I know you think your life started at birth and ends at the grave. In truth, the lifespan of your soul has been made up of many lifetimes. More than you can imagine. With this in mind, it is perfectly conceivable that the pain and struggles you endure now; the ones that puzzle and confound you; drive you to madness; stem from actions and behaviours from previous lives, brought into this lifetime by your soul.

With this understanding and awareness, just accept that the journey of your soul is beyond your current understanding.

Please know this, G-d is hard at work, shaping you, sculpting you and ultimately perfecting your soul. He doesn't demand your help in this regard but it is appreciated.

You likely were not told this:
Just as you stand by the Grand Canyon and speak into it and your voice echoes back to you; so too do all of your words and deeds in your lifetime echo back to you. They echo back even louder. This is an irrevocable law of the universe. With this in mind, choose to speak kind words, instead of insulting ones; choose to perform kind deeds instead of hasty ones.

To understand what is being said, you will have to tune out the words and tune into the energy behind them. The human language is, by its nature, an indirect form of communication. Precious few speak literally, directly and from the heart.

We must be ever so prudent when accepting critique, constructive criticism or viewpoints that might challenge our own. And we must try to always read between lines and examine not people's words but rather, their motivation.

To get to the root motivation of a particular word spoken or action taken, you might have to peel through more layers than are in an onion.

The energy of the soul which animates each one of us, is still the biggest mystery we know. It can't be measured -- or identified -- for it is a clandestine guest of this earthly realm.

Our brains give us the capability to tune-out the overload of information and knowledge that permeates the universe. It does this to avoid sensory overload and let us focus on the simple, static and mundane experience of living on this planet. A deeper consciousness awaits all of us as our soul makes its journey through the cosmos and realigns with the original source.

Sometimes putting your hands up and surrendering is the greatest victory of all.

If you can hear, see, feel, smell and touch, your creator can do no less. The power and depth of his senses are well beyond your realm of comprehension. This is what is known as the intelligence of the universe. The intelligence of the universe is a gateway to the mind of G-d.

There are times in your life when you will have to choose between two people you love very much. This is one of the tallest tasks this world will ask of you. So how can you win in such a horrible predicament? Make your choice and keep love in your heart for all parties concerned.

In a world enveloped by pain, anarchy and injustice, you are well within your rights to question the existence of a benevolent G-d. Draw a tiny drop of comfort in this: What appears as injustice to you now, will one day make perfect sense when you move beyond the chapter of your life and read the entire story of your soul.

Throughout your life you will be constantly misunderstood. Take solace my child, that G-d knows you for who you really are. For him, your soul is the FACE he stares at every day. Your heart and soul are the eyes he looks into with infinitely more love than your own parents.

Remember as you travel down the slope of one of life's valleys … When you reach the lowest point, the sun will no longer be visible. Without the sun's rays shining on your face, you will squirm and be overcome by fear and sadness. My child, don't be scared of being scared. We are all in the valley at one time or another. But in every valley, there is a secret treasure waiting to be unearthed. Perhaps many treasures.

You are all the sole arbiter of our own success. When you gaze inside yourself and find peace of mind, that is when you will truly know you have succeeded.

The foundation of human greatness is rooted in one's emotional capacity to help, heal and comfort others.

Human greatness is achieved in large measure by combining intellectual acuity with emotional intelligence. The bridge that joins the two is humility.

The arrogant man lives trapped in the walls of his own ego; a prisoner of his own selfishness. The humble man resides in the generosity of his own heart -- forever free.

My child, minions have stepped foot on earth and tried to fill the empty voids in their soul with material possessions. Folly to the man who embarks on this pursuit. The only way to avoid spiritual vacuity is to find meaning and purpose.

To find true meaning and a sense of deep purpose in this world, one must commit to being a marshal to the needs of another soul and to dutifully shepherd G-d's will.

Many organized religions have tainted and distorted G-d's will. Any religion that endorses or encourages conversion by sword, is not of G-d.

To man, physical war is a tantalizing proposition. To face the war inside himself, he would first have to find the enemy.

Do not be fooled when you stand in the midst of a large crowd and still you feel all alone. It is not until one is fully detached that they can become truly connected.

With enough dedication to a particular skill, we might just become masterful amongst our peers. But as good as you think you are, there is always someone more skilled. So then to reach your destiny, you will have to identify not just what you are skilled at but what you are extraordinarily gifted at. And then move forward, walking humbly with your gift.

As you climb the ladder to success, remember the pain and sacrifice that propelled you forward. You might try to convince yourself that your success was achieved on your own strength. How foolish is it to think that G-d was not an accomplice in your journey upward?

As you contemplate your own success, the natural question is: When so many hard working geniuses have failed before you, why have you been given this opportunity? The simple answer is: You were chosen because G-d had faith that once you reached the pinnacle, you would reach an outstretched arm to those climbing underneath you. By using your success to help others succeed, you will achieve a success far greater than anything you could have imagined.

All humans have their own unique way of communicating emotion. You may never hear your parents say "I Love You" but that does not mean that it was never said. Sometimes a pot of homemade soup as a greater expression of love than any word in the human language.

Don't aim to be an idol to others. Aim to be an inspiration.

At some point in your life you will probably have to choose between two people you love very much. This kind of predicament is almost unavoidable. If there is any solace to this quandary it is this: You will never have to choose between two G-ds. There is only one.

If the absence of something in your life does not have a major impact then its presence is of little significance. Sometimes we have to lose something to appreciate its true value in our life journey.

When I was 7 years-old, my family went to the corner store and left me alone for 5 minutes. I cried crocodile tears, for a thought I would never

see them again. When they returned, my tears somehow turned into chortles of laughter. Let this be a fitting analogy for the reality of life and death, as refracted through the human eye. We are all 7 year-olds, fearing that we will never see our loved ones again. When they return -- and they will -- your tears will also become bursts of laughter, just as mine did when my family returned home from the corner store.
Please keep your faith.

You will always prove your theory correct. Your mind is strong enough to prove even the most ridiculous hypothesis. As we travel through life and experience traumatic events, we often adopt beliefs that pivot around these horrible experiences. One of your most arduous tasks in this lifetime will be to change your negative beliefs into ones that hold promise and hope. Almost all of the influential leaders of the world did this to achieve their success. So must you.

When a moment of silence can be shared without awkwardness, one sits in the midst of a wonderful friendship.

Coincidence does not exist in the real world. It is just a word to explain what we cannot understand.

Because your enemy never teaches by design, it is his knowledge that is most valuable.

A leader has the courage to take the first step by himself but he never arrives at his destination alone.

Human greatness is embarking on an expedition to the furthest regions of your own heart. And then having the strength to share with the world what you have found.

Perhaps the world's single biggest epidemic is conformity. It is so dangerous because this malady does not attack the human body. Much worse than that -- it cripples the human spirit.

It is the absence of words that the most will always be said. Silence roars with emotion and the human eyes communicate what words can not.

Children are man's living blueprints, reminding us of who we once were. The elderly are man's breathing history books, showing us who we will be. Sad that they are such great teachers but we seldom listen to them.

The simpleton who is at peace with himself is the wisest of all.

Wise men control their anger because they know that the body and mind need calmness to soar.

The things in life that can not be seen or touched are the very things that we must choose to define us. For these intangibles are the only things can survive a concrete world.

Let love define you and you will eternally be *IN LOVE*.

A bond of love is stronger than the electrical grid of an entire continent. And as long as two beings have love in their hearts for one another, this relationship will fly through the cosmos on eternal wings.

The Power of Love
If two people can remember the inception of their relationship; when their love first sprung to life; then regardless of the passage of time, regardless of the pain endured, regardless of the physical distance between them, the love can survive against all odds.

If you go back far enough in time, there is a point where all of our tools and resources to gauge, measure, interpret and understand the cosmos -- break down. Anything that is derived from this world, is useless in understanding what happens outside it. Therefore we can not penetrate the mind of G-d. The one solace for us human beings is that we can get a tiny glimpse of the heart of G-d, should we dare to sit still and listen to our own soul.

The laws of nature say if the heart is fully and completely committed, then success is academic.

Most people fail not because of what others do to them, but what they do to themselves.

My friends, we are all master storytellers when it comes to conjuring an exciting narrative of our life. Be bold and challenge the authenticity of your story. The story that you have been telling yourself, over and over again, may be completely wrong. If you are humble enough to ask G-d to testify to the truth of your story, you might just find that your story -- compelling though it was -- lacked empirical truth. And only G-d's empirical truth can set you free. Press into G-d for the truth.

My child, the difficult times of your life, are the times when your soul achieves most of its growth. So then when you speak to G-d, it would be most prudent to ask him not for a painless life but for the resilience to endure a life of tribulation.

G-d does not present you with a test that is beyond your threshold or tolerance. There is a big difference between how strong you think you are and how strong G-d knows you are. You are much stronger than you can ever imagine.

G-d has never been asked a question and withheld the answer. But human beings often ask a question and then turn a deaf ear.

Avoid the company of cynical, pessimistic people. Avoid them like you avoid toxic fumes. For once you inhale them, you might spend a lifetime trying to clear these toxins from your lungs. And believe me, cynicism is toxic. Don't ever confuse cynicism with practicality. You can be practical and still be optimistic about the infinite possibilities that exist and about the promise of a good outcome.

Never let anybody impose their definition of success onto you until you have lived long enough to know what success is.

Being able to distinguish the difference between guilt and regret will literally add years to your life. Guilt is an absolute destructive force with no redeeming value. It torments you and eats away at your very own flesh. Regret on the other hand, is an absolute constructive force. It takes the disappointment you have with yourself and creates an intention to change. Choose regret.

Your *EGO* is the biggest stumbling block to acquiring intelligence. A wise man will ask many questions and give very few answers. Wisdom is built by disregarding how silly you may look for asking foolish questions.

If only you understood the power of your tongue. Its reach and impact is so vast, that souls are irrevocably wounded by its swiftness and nations are destroyed by its acidity. Conversely, its power to build, grow, bless, heal and comfort is limitless.

Silence is worth two coins. And words are worth one. Do not be afraid of silence, for G-d's voice projects best in the stillness of time. Like everything in life, silence is a fabric with many layers. The deeper the silence, the greater the opportunity to reach the truth of the cosmos.

One poor decision in one generation can put into motion a domino effect that will run through many generations and sometimes ... even centuries.

The young should always be open to the wisdom of the elderly. Conversely, the elderly should always be open to the guidance of the young. Together, their dialogue touches all crevices of the circle of life.

Parents, no matter how much damage you have done to your children, know that you can heal them with love, regret and apology. Time does not heal all wounds. Only love can.

It is easy to give when your bank account is overflowing but it can be excruciating to give when you are down to your last few pennies. So then a person's true generosity can be determined only when he is poor.

The highest level of giving is giving done in private. Not true -- the highest level of giving is giving anonymously.

The louder your voice gets, the less audible you become. The angrier you get, the weaker you become -- in every way.

Unforgiveness is like dropping a 5 ton anchor in the middle of the ocean. No matter how much nascent greatness you possess, you're stuck in the middle of nowhere. Until you can forgive, you will only see dry land in the distance but never step foot on it.

Knowledge will always speak in the idiom of its times but wisdom is *TIMELESS*.

Be ever so weary when hearing second hand information. Invariably, the truth becomes horribly distorted as it changes hands.

When you are engaged in dialogue that you deem important: Pay close attention to what is not said, for it reveals much about the speaker and the nature of the conversation. Ambiguity is the ocean where every charlatan swims.

Nelson Mandela was a true humanitarian for one reason. He was willing to live in inhumane conditions so others would not have to. This earth of ours literally spins on this kind of self-sacrifice.

The pinnacle of foolishness is to try to refute the existence of the supernatural while existing in a natural environment.

It is virtually immeasurable how much time and energy you have wasted by trying to impress others. The mind boggles at the success that would find you, if you stopped trying to win the approval of others and started trying to win your own self-respect.

Some of the world's greatest inventions were born from contentious debate. Debate your opponent to elevate an idea to its highest point. Folly to the man who debates only to win rather than to find the truth.

If the world really is a stage ... perhaps G-d just wants us all to play ourselves, instead of pretending to be someone we are not.

If you realize in your heart you are wrong, don't walk but run to make a sincere apology. This single act will save you and everybody around you much heartache.

If insanity is doing the same thing over and over and expecting a different result ... Can we all agree that the story of human civilization is the story of complete and utter insanity?

When you look into the eyes of your dog, contemplate the likelihood that he or she is the one caring for you. And not the other way around. The soul of a dog is that pure.

Every great leader has a siamese twin and his/her name is: Loneliness.

If ignorance is bliss, what value is there to be wise? Wisdom comes with a price. But the world can't exist without it. All of that said, you will only start to understand this world through the faculty of your heart. When it becomes closed, so too does the pipeline to all knowledge, wisdom and truth.

The world will pervert even the purest idea; it will taint the most noble act; it will question the worthiest aspiration. Know that your sincerity will win you many fans but it will also attract many haters. Never let this reality stop you from showing this cruel world the true colours of your heart.

If you can't be happy for the success of others, you will never be happy with your own.

When you have a strong reaction to another human being, this always points back to your *OWN* fears and insecurities. Be very careful before discarding these people just because they make you feel a little uncomfortable. G-d and the universe will use other people to expose your weaknesses. Sometimes the mirrors in our home become fogged and we need a perfect stranger to show up and be the mirror that cuts through the haze and sends us back our true reflection. What a gift of love this is.

The wise man knows that all humans are interconnected. With this knowledge he will then pause at the slightest sight of suffering. He will surely rejoice at the sight of joy and laughter around him. For his neighbours victories are really his very own victories and his neighbours sadness is really his own sadness. The separation that exists from one man to another is a great illusion. For we are one.

How ironic that a human being coins the term 'artificial intelligence?' Is this to say that the intelligence of a human being has a base-reality?

When you see a person who possesses a particular skill or attribute that is superior to yours, this will trigger a base human response. The dark side of you will be inclined to shoot the person down. The divine side of you will seek to study and learn the ways of that individual. The thing that gets in the way of the careful study of that which is superior is ego, pride and laziness. Resist shooting down a brother in envy and strive to humbly learn in his ways.

Everybody wants to be blessed but few understand the immense responsibility that accompanies their blessing.

When you pray for your dreams to come true, make sure you include a prayer for the maturity, strength and responsibility to receive it -- and carry it.

Few Hollywood actors are worthy of your admiration. The beggar on the street might very well be more worthy. It is also true that the many panhandlers are oscar-worthy thespians. Not for you to judge.

Don't let the futility of social dynamics sour you from the benefits of religion. And more importantly, don't confuse religion with G-d. Just because man has distorted the word of G-d does not mean that G-d does not exist.

A wise man knows when to let a deadly fire burn itself out and when to intervene and extinguish it aggressively.

A multitasker is usually good at many things but great at nothing.

Your ego will get in the way of much spiritual progress -- if you let it.

Opportunity knocks but we often pretend nobody's home.

Get out of your head and into your heart, as soon as possible.

The best way to find love is to offer it first.

Preconceived notions have killed many worthy dreams.

GET OUT OF YOUR WAY

What if we could go into a given situation with no prior thought to our own needs and desires? And let G-d and his universe show us what they want for us and what they want from us. How would this kind of patience, trust and faith affect the possibility of us acquiring the deepest needs of our soul ... and offering others the needs of their soul?

Most people that end up backed into a corner are there because they were trying too hard to do it alone. Think about it: It's hard to be backed into a corner when you are walking hand in hand with other people.

Many people fail because they did not team up with the right people. The greatest decision you will ever make in your life is who you want to be your life partner. Choose wisely.

A great intellect that has not yet been humbled is both tragic and lethal. In fact, a bitter intellectual is like a serial killer on the loose.

What you *do* and *say*, when nobody is around to bear witness, is in essence the measurement of your true character. Your visceral, knee-jerk reactions to life, bespeak much about the contents of your heart and soul.

Most of us do not understand the extraordinary power of speech. With the gift of words, G-d made us all iconic land developers. Many of us never get beyond digging holes. While others erect skyscrapers that reach literally all the way to the heavens. We all speak in haste but just understand that your words carry the ability to resuscitate the weary and the ability to demolish the triumphant. Every word out of your mouth echoes back to you.

The truth has an emotional arch all of its own. It usually starts with anger and resistance and curves all the way around to love and gratitude. The truth is the great liberator of all life.

No need to run from your own emotions. Your salty tears are more beautiful than any earthly waterfall or any glistening wave in the roaring ocean.

True wisdom starts and ends at the ability and willingness to say: I don't know.

In the way you live your life, you will preach a non-verbal sermon to the world. However, the content of your message is completely reliant on the sensibility of the onlooker. To the bitter and envious, your sermon will be full of contradictions and hypocrisy. To the joyful and grateful, your sermon will offer inspiration and many wonderful lessons.

You will never please the mind of a cynic. Trying to win the approval of a cynical person is like shoveling dirt into a black hole and hoping that it eventually fills.

Many human beings have enjoyed a rebirth by morphing cynicism into caution -- and fear into concern.

We inflict much anxiety onto ourselves by overloading our brains with decisions that we can't seem to make. Should I or shouldn't I do this? Should I or shouldn't I do that? All of the decisions that overwhelm you in your life funnel into one singular decision: Will you choose **LOVE** or **FEAR**?

It fascinates me that a religion that starts out in love, can be so quickly twisted into a religion of fear by the craftiness of human hands.

People often think their calling is what comes most naturally to them. Sometimes one's calling is something that comes with great difficulty. Many people don't realize their true calling in life because they retreat at the first sign of resistance.

When an airplane ascends into the air -- unfailingly -- it hits an altitude where it faces incredible resistance by nature. Every plane that makes a trip somewhere, has to overcome a unique threshold, where gravity, the plane and the wind currents all fight against each other. So too, will you have to overcome a similar threshold to achieve your true calling on this earth.

The Illusion of Life and Death
Life and death do not exist as you think they do. Let's take a look at the birth process. In the womb, a baby's lungs are completely contracted. And NO blood goes to those lungs. The child has a hole in its heart.

It is completely submerged under water. All details of the anatomy and physiology of a baby in the womb are lethal ingredients for survival in the outside world. As the unborn baby travels from the womb to the entrance of this world, it is on its way to a sure death. How can it survive as it leaves an environment that is completely antithetical to the one it is moving towards? It can't. And it doesn't. In fact, in strictly medical terms, upon entry to this world every newborn baby dies for a second or two. Yep. Ask your doctor. The baby even turns blue and then purple. As expected, it breaks down in transition. But in a mesmerizing turn of events, in a matter of mere seconds, all functions that were in exact concert reverse themselves. The blood vessel that is taking blood away from the lungs clamps down. At that point the blood is forced into the pulmonary circulation (the lungs). As the blood hits the lungs they pop open. At that moment the child takes its first breath. And a minute later the child is doing just fine, fully adapted to a new environment. Now that must have taken a few million years to happen by accident! We seldom think about this process and how mind blowing it really is. Yet we all went through it. The truth is, every last one of us went from resting comfortably in our Mother's womb, to death and then back to life. Not the life we came from but a new kind of existence, one we could not have imagined as our Mothers carried us. My friends, meditate on this transition that happens at birth. For this miracle represents the true power of G-d. And the true power of the universe he created. It also profoundly speaks to the idea that life and death are words us human animals use to cover up our gross ignorance to the journey of the soul and the constant transitions of existence. In reality, you are neither alive or dead. You just exist. No matter what form and no matter what realm -- you exist. And always will. This should not encourage you to rest on your laurels as you traverse planet earth. You can exist with pain or joy. How you behave in this lifetime, ultimately inflicts significant amounts of joy and pain unto your soul. The extent to which your actions will affect your soul is not certain. We only now that there is an effect. Please consider this very carefully.

Our Furry Friends

The source of your existence is love. G-d is love in its purest, most coarse and powerful form. You can not begin to fathom the immensity of G-d and his love. You don't have the faculty to comprehend it. The closest you will get to understanding G-d's love in this lifetime is when you completely submit all of your heart to another being. You don't need to be a parent to completely submit all of your love. But it might just be the most natural way for us humans to do it. In lieu of this, you can submit your hearts full capacity to another living thing that needs you to survive and flourish. Some people establish deep soulful bonds with their dogs. And a bond between man and *man's best friend* should not be overlooked or underestimated in any way. These bonds can be every bit as loving -- and sometimes more loving than the bonds that exist between two human beings. While it is true that we express our love in the physical world through verbal/ non verbal communication and physical actions, the roots of a loving bond are *purely spiritual*. Love is a force. Love is an energy. It can manifest physically but it resonates *FROM* and returns *TO* the spiritual realm -- always. It's interesting that we think of dogs as inferior creatures to us humans because they are for the most part submissive to our grand designs. Just because something submits does not mean it is inferior in any way. There is much we don't understand about the soul of a dog. In fact we understand little about the soul of humans. And thus we must be ever so careful not to miss opportunities to learn from the pure motivations and natural instincts of our furry friends. In Hebrew the word for dog is *Kelev*. Translated to English *Kelev* means *All Heart*. A dog is all heart. Since true understanding comes from the faculty of the heart, a dog understands much more than you might realize.

You are ready to be here.

Ieden Wall is an award winning TV Host, Comic, Author and Motivational Speaker. He travels the globe, speaking about his own personal story of survival; going from a 15 year-old welfare kid, living on his own, to an acclaimed writer and media personality. These days Wall spends a large chunk of time speaking to large groups on how to use humour to overcome crises and triumph over adversity. He has an insatiable desire to pass on his wisdom to all who seek personal growth and enlightenment. The Toronto-born writer is already hard at work on Volume #2 in his Wisdom of Wall series. To contact Mr. Wall directly or to inquire about booking him to speak at your next event, please visit www.edentv.ca

Thanks to the following people who made this book possible:

Judy Skopit
Teddy Lambersky
Sophie Despotopoulos
Grace Goheen
Patti Seward
Jack Wall

Proof

Made in the USA
Columbia, SC
17 November 2017